A Guide to Surviving a Career in Academia

Navigating an academic career is a complex process – to be successful requires mastering several "rites of passage." This comprehensive guide takes academics at all stages of their career through a journey, beginning at graduate school and ending with retirement.

Written from a feminist perspective, it draws on the information offered in workshops conducted at national meetings like the American Society of Criminology and the Society for the Study of Social Problems. Through the course of the book an expert team of authors guide you through the obstacle course of finding effective mentors during graduate school, finding a job, negotiating a salary, teaching, collaborating with practitioners, successfully publishing, earning tenure and redressing denial, and, finally, retirement.

This collection is a "must read" for all academics, but especially women just beginning their career, who face unique challenges when navigating through these age-old rites of passage.

Emily Lenning is an Assistant Professor of Criminal Justice at Fayetteville State University. Her areas of interest include state crime, the social construction of deviance, media representations of crime and justice, and transgender issues. Her most current work explores the systematic and mass rapes of Nigerian women at the hands of state-endorsed military groups and the problematic nature of gendered language. **Sara Brightman** is a PhD candidate at Western Michigan University. Her areas of interest broadly include feminist theory, global feminism, feminist criminology, state-corporate crime as well as feminist epistemology and methodology. Recent projects have focused on state violence by police against women in Pakistan, and state-corporate violence against women in Nigeria. **Susan Caringella** is an internationally known expert on rape, feminism, and criminology. She has published in academic journals and written books on topics ranging from rape to violence against women, legislative change, sociological, criminological and feminist theory, political ideology and public opinion. Her work has been widely cited and recognized with national, state, and university scholarship awards and honours.

A Guide to Surviving a Career in Academia

Navigating the rites of passage

Edited by
**Emily Lenning, Sara Brightman,
and Susan Caringella**

LONDON AND NEW YORK

First published 2011
by Routledge
2 Park Square, Milton Park, Abingdon, Oxon, OX14 4RN

Simultaneously published in the USA and Canada
by Routledge
270 Madison Avenue, New York, NY 10016

Routledge is an imprint of the Taylor & Francis Group, an informa business

Typeset in Sabon by Taylor & Francis Books
Printed and bound in Great Britain by CPI Antony Rowe, Chippenham,
Wiltshire.

British Library Cataloguing in Publication Data
A catalogue record for this book is available from the British Library

Library of Congress Cataloging in Publication Data
A guide to surviving a career in academia : navigating the rites of passage/
edited by Emily Lenning, Sara Brightman, and Susan Caringella.
    p. cm.
    1. College teachers–United States. 2. Universities and colleges–United
    States–Faculty. 3. College teaching–Vocational guidance–United States.
    4. Women college teachers–United Sates. 5. Feminism and education.
    I. Lenning, Emily. II. Brightman, Sara. III. Caringella, Susan.
LB1778.2.G84 2010
378.1'2023–dc22
2010006039

ISBN: 978-0-415-78021-6 (hbk)
ISBN: 978-0-415-78022-3 (pbk)
ISBN: 978-0-203-85590-4 (ebk)

Contents

About the authors

Carolyn Rebecca Block is a Senior Research Analyst at the Illinois Criminal Justice Information Authority, where she advises policy makers, researchers, and the public on the use and interpretation of data, especially measurement issues and violence prevention. A founder of the Homicide Research Working Group, she is principal investigator of the Chicago Women's Health Risk Study (CWHRS), a large longitudinal study of lethal and nonlethal intimate partner violence. Working closely with the Chicago Police Department, she has collected and maintained the Chicago Homicide Dataset (CHD) since 1965. Her current research focuses on collaborative analyses of the CHD and the CWHRS.

Sara Brightman is an instructor at Fayetteville State University. Her areas of interest broadly include feminist theory, global feminism, feminist criminology, state corporate crime as well as feminist epistemology and methodology. Past research has been on third wave feminist identity, women's professional networking, and backlash against feminism. More recent projects have been on state violence by police against women in Pakistan and state corporate violence, specifically rape by security forces, against women in Nigeria. Her current research focuses on victimology and sexual violence by U.S. agencies.

Susan Caringella is an internationally known expert on rape, feminism, and criminology. Her work has been widely cited and recognized, with national, state, and university scholarship awards and honors. She was honored as Distinguished Scholar by the Division on Women and Crime of the American Society of Criminology in 1998. She was previously recognized by a Division on Critical Criminology Lifetime Achievement Award in 1993. She published *Addressing Rape Reform in Law and Practice* in 2009 and is working on *Rape: 2,000 Years and Counting*.

Deshonna Collier-Goubil is a doctoral candidate in the Department of Sociology and Anthropology at Howard University. Her research areas are urban sociology, criminology, and race/class/gender studies. In addition, she holds a Master's degree in theology from Fuller Graduate Schools in California, where her studies focused on black theologies and the urban Church. Deshonna is a research assistant at the National Institute of Justice and her dissertation research looks at the effects of neighborhood character-istics on intimate partner violence, using spatial analysis. Being active in the university's community, Deshonna serves as the Graduate Student Council president, is a member of the Organization of Graduate Sociologists, and is a member of the Edward Alexander Bouchet Graduate Honor Society.

Mona J. E. Danner is Professor of Sociology and Criminal Justice and Director of the PhD program in Criminology and Criminal Justice at Old Dominion University. Her research and teaching interests are in the areas of social inequalities (gender, race/ethnicity, class), crime control policies, and globa-lization. For more than a decade she has been engaged in research and con-ducted workshops on gender and the process of negotiating academic contracts. Danner is the author of more than twenty-five academic journal articles and book chapters and has presented her research at conferences throughout the United States, Europe and at the NGO Forum held in con-junction with the UN Conference on Women in 1995 in Beijing. In 1997 she received the New Scholar Award from the Division on Women and Crime of the American Society of Criminology.

Kristi Holsinger is an Associate Professor of Criminal Justice and Criminology at the University of Missouri. Since 1995 she has been involved in research focusing on the needs and experiences of system-involved girls. She has written articles on innovative teaching strategies in mentoring incar-cerated youth and teaching restorative justice to traditional college students and incarcerated youth. Her research interests focus on correctional policies and programs for women, girls, and youth mentoring programs. Holsinger was awarded the Department of Sociology/Criminal Justice and Crimino-logy's Outstanding Teaching Award in 2004. She also received the Outstanding Teaching Award of the College of Arts and Sciences in 2005.

Emily Lenning is an assistant professor of criminal justice at Fayetteville State University. Her areas of interest include state crime, the social con-struction of deviance, media representations of crime and justice, and trans-gender issues. Her most current work explores the systematic mass rapes of Nigerian women at the hands of state-endorsed military groups and the problematic nature of gendered language. She has been an active member of the Division on Women and Crime of the American Society of Criminology for several years, serving as a member of the executive board and as the chair of various committees.

Kate Luther is an assistant professor of sociology at Pacific Lutheran University. She received her PhD in 2008 from the University of California, Riverside.

Her research and teaching interests include women's imprisonment, intimate partner violence, and juvenile delinquency. For the past three years she has served as co-chair of the Student Affairs Committee of the American Society of Criminology's Division on Women and Crime. In this position she helped to develop a mentoring program for graduate students and organized the "Strategies for Success on the Job Market" workshop at the annual meeting. Kate herself went on the job market last year and is now part of a hiring committee at her new institution.

Angela M. Moe is an Associate Professor of Sociology, with affiliated appointment in Gender and Women's Studies, at Western Michigan University. Her areas of specialization are in feminist criminology and sociology, specifically violence against women, gendered criminalization, and holistic health. Her work has appeared in such journals as *Violence Against Women*, *Women and Criminal Justice*, *Journal of Contemporary Ethnography*, *Journal of Interpersonal Violence*, *Women and Therapy*, and *Women's Studies Quarterly*. Her research investigates the links between women's disembodiment (through victimization, illness, and the like) and the healing aspects of movement. Angela organized and facilitated the New Faculty Workshop at the annual American Society of Criminology meetings from 2003 to 2006.

Angela Moore is the Associate Deputy Director for Research and Evaluation at the National Institute of Justice (NIJ), U.S. Department of Justice. Dr. Moore is also an adjunct faculty at the University of Maryland, University College. Prior to her appointment as Associate Deputy Director she served as the Chief of the Violence and Victimization Research Division and directed NIJ's Violence against Women and Family Violence Research and Evaluation Program. Prior to joining NIJ, Moore taught at the University of Maryland and worked in human resources at the Federal Bureau of Prisons in New York City. She received her PhD in criminology from the University of Maryland and her B.S. and M.P.A. degrees from Pennsylvania State University.

Kristine Mullendore, JD, is a Professor in the School of Criminal Justice/Legal Studies Program at Grand Valley State University and has been a member of the State Bar of Michigan, since 1977. Prior to her academic career she worked for more than twelve years as an assistant prosecuting attorney for Kent County, Michigan, and taught for five years at Montcalm Community College. She has published several journal articles and presented papers on a diverse range of topics relating to the criminal and civil aspects of the U.S. legal system. She is serving as chair of the Executive Committee of the University Academic Senate at Grand Valley.

Lisa M. Murphy is an assistant professor of criminal justice at California State University. Her areas of specialization are in the intersection of criminology and gender, especially as they relate to juvenile delinquency and intimate partner violence. Within these broad fields, her research and teaching examine how being a victim of violence (in the home and in the larger community) influences the risk of being involved in violence throughout the life course. Lisa organized and facilitated the New Faculty Workshop at the annual American Society of Criminology meetings from 2007 to 2008.

Winifred L. Reed is Chief of the Crime Control and Prevention Research Division, Office of Research and Evaluation, at the National Institute of Justice. She is responsible for managing the research and evaluation portfolios of the division, including those in policing, crime mapping, and crime prevention. She has worked in a wide range of substantive areas during her thirty-plus years of experience at NIJ, including law enforcement, Indian country crime and justice, gangs, school-based programs, criminal careers, criminal behavior, and crime prevention. Reed received her B.A. and M.A. degrees from the American University.

Claire M. Renzetti is Professor of Sociology at the University of Dayton. She is editor of the international, interdisciplinary journal *Violence Against Women*, co-editor of the Interpersonal Violence book series for Oxford University Press, and editor of the Gender, Crime, and Law book series for Northeastern University Press. She has authored or edited sixteen books and numerous book chapters, journal articles, and other publications, primarily in the area of violence against women.

Suzanna M. Rose is Senior Associate Dean for the Sciences and Professor of Psychology and Women's Studies at Florida International University. She has published extensively on issues related to women, including personal relationships and professional networks. She readily incorporates feminist activism into her teaching and also her work as a consultant concerning strategic career planning for women in academe.

Susan F. Sharp received her PhD in sociology from the University of Texas in 1996. She is a Professor in the Department of Sociology and in the Department of Women's Studies at the University of Oklahoma. She was formerly chair of the Division on Women and Crime of the American Society of Criminology. In 2006 Sharp launched the journal *Feminist Criminology* as its founding editor. She is the editor of *The Incarcerated Woman* (2003), author of a book on the effects of the death penalty on families of offenders, *Hidden Victims* (2005), and author of more than thirty articles and book chapters focusing on gender, nationality, crime, and the criminal justice system. She has received numerous awards, including the 2005 Good Teaching Award from the University of Oklahoma and both the Kenneth Crook and the Rufus G. Hall faculty awards from the College of Liberal Studies at the University of Oklahoma. Since 2005 she has conducted the annual Oklahoma Study of Incarcerated Women and their Children for the Oklahoma Commission on Children and Youth, resulting in reports to the state legislature and policy changes.

Nancy A. Wonders is Professor and chair of the Department of Criminology and Criminal Justice at Northern Arizona University. She is a past chair of the American Society of Criminology's Division on Women and Crime, has served on the editorial board of *Criminology* and *Feminist Criminology*, and is a recipient of the Western Society of Criminology's June Morrison–Tom Gitchoff Award for significant improvement of the quality of justice. Her research and teaching focus on the relation between social inequality, difference, and justice, with an emphasis on underrepresented and vulnerable populations, and she has produced numerous publications on these themes. Over the past two decades she has served on a search committee almost every year. She has also mentored others about the job search process at her own university and at workshops at professional associations.

Introduction
The journey

A journey of a thousand miles must begin with a single step.

(Lao Tzu)

A career in academia is like a road trip. Graduate school marks the beginning of your journey and retirement the end, with countless stops along the way. We all hope that our journey is smooth and we reach our destination unharmed, but without careful planning and some good advice, you might find yourself taking far too many detours. The purpose of this book is to help you navigate around those detours. Throughout your career you will face multiple rites of passage, each of which are represented by a chapter in this book.

The genesis for this book owes primarily to the Division on Women and Crime (DWC) of the American Society of Criminology (ASC). Some of us began, years ago, conducting workshops on the types of concerns found in these chapters, and they have been continuing for years, e.g., the workshop on securing tenure has been mounted at the ASC and sponsored by the DWC for well over a decade now. These kinds of workshops have proliferated over the years from within not only the DWC but more recently from the Division on People of Color and Crime of the ASC and have come to grow as well in other professional associations, such as the Society for the Study of Social Problems. The DWC expressed interest a few years ago in collecting and publishing some of the tips and advice the various workshops proffered over these different venues and conferences. Here we draw together articles penned by a number of the workshop leaders as we somewhat artificially craft the series of strategies/ workshops on an academic career into the flowing 'journey' we posit to characterize the road to scholarly success.

The first step on this journey is surviving graduate school, and it is a serious rite of passage as the gateway to an academic profession. It will always be challenging and, at times, rewarding. It feels like a never-ending journey, with speed bumps, hairpin turns, and obstacles the whole way. A centerpiece of this experience is the relationships you have with faculty, fellow graduate students and, importantly, friends and loved ones. Strengthening these relationships will help you survive the rites of passage that all graduate students must face – classes, seminars, research, comprehensive exams, and theses/ dissertations. Chapter 1, "Surviving graduate school," discusses the importance of these relationships as well as how to maintain and build them. Strategies for successfully passing the comprehensive exams and timely completion of theses/ dissertations are offered.

The next rite of passage is beginning the "career itself," stepping into the job market. Chapter 2, "Strategies for success on the job market," will help you prepare for living your life as a job candidate. Although it seems a long way off during your first year of graduate school, preparing yourself for the job hunt begins immediately. This chapter provides advice so you know what you should be doing (and collecting) in graduate school to be a success on the job market. The chapter delineates how to search for open positions and goes forward to walk you through the process, such as what types of materials it is advantageous to include in your application package. This chapter will also help you to prepare for the interview process as well as to find the way to best distinguish yourself in the sea of applicants.

Once you have interviewed and secured a job offer you'll be ready to hit the ground running, right? Not so fast. An important step, and one that can have a significant impact on your salary for the rest of your life, is negotiating the job contract and, importantly, your salary. The negotiation process can be intimidating, especially because you are relieved just to have found a job. Chapter 3, "Money matters," addresses the need for developing strategies to negotiate your first academic job contract. Particular attention is paid to gender differences in negotiations and why it is so important for you to become knowledgeable early on.

Now that you have secured the job offer and negotiated your job contract, the next step in your journey is navigating being a new faculty member. As recent graduates, many new faculty experience new issues emanating from this move, some of which are specific to women. Every university and department has its own history and politics to navigate, which can be troubling waters for someone new to them. Chapter 4, "Being a new faculty," discusses ways to adapt to this change in status and provides advice on balancing teaching, research and service, as well as developing a professional–personal balance. As is true in all stages of your career, being in the know and knowing the right people can be a significant advantage to any new faculty member.

For some women pursuing an academic career, teaching can be the most enjoyable and rewarding part of the job. However, teaching experience during graduate school can be incredibly varied, from being a teaching assistant working with a professor to an instructor with your own course. Regardless of the graduate experience, we all can benefit from learning more about teaching and pedagogy. Chapter 5, "Teaching with intention," discusses teaching techniques for creating an active and engaging classroom. In addition, it offers tips for continuing to develop yourself as a dynamic and innovative teacher.

Many academics are familiar with the phrase "publish or perish." Certainly publishing is a significant rite of passage in every academic's career, as it is a requirement for tenure and promotion in most (if not all) colleges and universities. Chapter 6, "A brief guide to academic publishing," provides step-by-step advice on different avenues of publishing. Publishing in a journal requires preparation and the ability to handle rejection; both of these concerns are addressed in this chapter. Publishing or editing a book has its own challenges, so it is important to be informed about the process early on.

As you continue to navigate the rites of passage in your career you may find the desire to embark on new research projects that "make a difference" and to conduct research which requires data to which you may not have immediate access. Chapter 7, "Collaborating with practitioners," addresses the benefits of collaborative research, as well as providing advice that academic researchers and practitioners can utilize to complete successful collaborative research projects.

Navigating the many passages of an academic career culminates in going up for and (hopefully) getting tenure. Chapter 8, "Getting tenure and redressing denial," provides advice on the tenure process, including what you should be doing in the years leading up to your tenure review. Knowing what to do when problems arise during the tenure process is often difficult to navigate, and this chapter discusses the options you have. Of course, there are also specific problems that can arise for women during tenure review, which are considered separately here.

Chapter 9, "Retirement," covers the final topic, but retirement is by no means the end of the journey. Discussions of retirement frequently focus in on financial planning, but this chapter goes further to discuss the emotional process of retirement. Acknowledging what you will be giving up following your academic career and finding ways to replace and refill your life are important things to think about when approaching retirement. Reflection on, and the pursuit of, hobbies, interests, and volunteer opportunities is one way to address retirement. Yet, as with the other steps of this journey, no advice is one-size-fits-all. However, this chapter traces pathways for each of us to think about while continuing the journey in various alternative directions once we retire from our academic careers.

It is probably tempting to read only the chapters of this book that sound like they apply to your position in this journey, but we encourage you to take a few steps back and start at the beginning. What we hope will become clear is that, no matter where you are on this long road trip, mentoring is key to your success and the success of others. The original purpose of the book, of course, was to provide sound advice to help you navigate through your own career. The purpose that has become more salient through its writing, however, is for you to be equipped to help others navigate their careers as well. You begin this book as a mere tourist, but our goal is to make you a tour guide.

As one of us has always said in opening one of these workshops, your first job is to get and keep your job! To do that you need to map out your career goals and means of achieving them, i.e., to chart your plan for securing, keeping, and growing in, your career. Most of us will take the time to plan just about everything but that; we organize, gain knowledge, muster resources, draft, revise, edit, and set aside blocks of time for a research project, a term paper, a conference presentation, a publication, our service/engagement with various communities, time/dates with family and friends, and on and on. Yet few of us even contemplate what/where we want be when we "grow up," how we want to be known, what we want to be known for, and/or what a successful career, one juxtaposed with a full life, would look like. Ironically, it is precisely this that should be done first (and regularly revisited) in order to ensure the greatest odds for the best successes. It is to this task that we now turn. Bon voyage!

1   Surviving graduate school

Sara Brightman and Emily Lenning

Graduate school can be both the most painful and the most rewarding thing you will ever do in your life. It seems like an endless stream of hurdles; as soon as you survive one, another is set before you. When we survived the thesis defense at the MA level we were sure that it was the hardest thing we would ever do but, much to our dismay, we found later that it was a rather mundane accomplishment. Months and months of work culminated with a pat on the back and the realization that ahead of us were comprehensive exams and, of course, the dreaded dissertation. We took both of the required comprehensive exams (called "area exams" in our neck of the woods) within the span of a few months, all while teaching and taking courses of our own. Once again, months and months of preparation were rewarded with nothing more than a proverbial thumbs-up and questions about when our dissertations would be done. The dissertation, of course, felt like it took forever to finish, though it didn't. As we will discuss later, and as you will see reiterated as you progress through this book, a career in academia is defined by a multitude of rites of passage. In fact, being successful in graduate school requires the recognition that the comprehensive exams, the dissertation, and all the other hurdles of graduate school are minute in the grand scheme of things. Those who forget this end up taking decades to finish their degrees, which ultimately defeats the purpose of graduate school. Graduate school is but a stepping-stone to a greater goal. Most people who choose to endure doctoral level education hold the ultimate goal of being a professional academic of some sort; if you spend half of your working age obtaining the degree, you have thrown away half of your career opportunities. Thus, it is imperative that graduate students are given the skills to progress through their programs quickly and effectively.

The journey

Graduate education has a history dating back more than 700 years (Mauch and Burch 1998). Still in the United States less than 9 percent of people complete a graduate degree of any sort (Bauman and Graf 2003). There are many factors that contribute to this, but the overwhelming prospect of the work ahead is enough to deter many.

As recent graduates and new faculty, we hope to use our own experiences to help you navigate through your graduate program, because, after all, it is the entry rite of passage in your career. This chapter is about how we have endured the past five years and, hopefully, how others can make it through as well. Merely surviving graduate school requires a tremendous amount of support and surviving *successfully* means that you have forged relationships that will help foster your future career (i.e., friendships and mentorships), that you have the skills to master the comprehensive exams, and that you can make it through your thesis and dissertation in a timely manner. Though these are not the only challenges of graduate school they are perhaps the biggest, and what follows is what has worked for us and, hopefully, what you can make work for yourself.

Making friends

You may ask yourself, what do friends have to do with making it through graduate school? The answer is – everything. Having a cohort of academic friends, one created through your department or one that you have created, is imperative to your success and sanity (Rossman 2002). Throughout this chapter you will hear us describe many of our experiences collectively because both of us came from the same department at roughly the same time – Emily is only one year ahead of Sara in her career and both of our interests coincide. The relationship we share has made a tremendous difference in trying to navigate graduate school. We have experienced many hurdles simultaneously, and when Emily's experiences preceded Sara's, Sara was able to learn from Emily's mistakes. Working together has prevented us from making one of the biggest mistakes of graduate school – reinventing the wheel. Though you will feel like you are the only person to ever tackle such a feat, you are only one of many before you, and to ignore that is academic suicide. If you do not purposely seek out experiences of others, you risk making mistakes that someone could have easily warned you about – mistakes that will delay your graduation from student status. Trust us, no one wants to make graduate school any longer than it has to be.

Beyond helping you navigate the rites of passage in graduate school, friends are someone to lean on when times get rough. Even though you already have friends and family that you love dearly, the fact of the matter is that some of your experiences will only be truly understood by other graduate students. The greatest evidence of this will probably be when you take your first comprehensive exam. You will spend months preparing (as will be discussed later), only to have all of your work boil down to one day or perhaps a week of writing to save your life. Your nonacademic friends may be sympathetic that you have to take a "big test," but that's probably where their understanding will end. Your cohort will recognize that for that one day or one week you feel like your life depends on your ability to put together thought-provoking, coherent sentences under immense pressure. Only other graduate students will understand when you are so stressed out that you find yourself crying in the middle of the hallway after having read seven books in one day – and they certainly won't brush the incident off as mere anxiety over a menial "test." This may seem unimportant now, but in the first moment one of your cohort says "I understand" (and they mean it) you will realize why this empathy is imperative to your survival.

Nevertheless, even though your academic friends can empathize and be there to say a sincere "Cheers" whenever you successfully jump a hurdle, they are, simply, a support system. Obviously people cannot teach you what they don't know about, so it is important to find mentors who have already beaten the game, so to speak. Thus, once you have built yourself an army of good friends, it's time to find a mentor (or two, or three, or four).

Finding a mentor

Identifying a mentor early on in your program is of primary importance to your success in graduate school and beyond (Kunselman et al. 2003; Marshall and Green 2004). However, finding a mentor is more difficult than it sounds. As much as departments would like you to believe that they are filled with eager professors ready to help you through your degree, it simply is not the case. The truth is you may find yourself surrounded by professors who are busy jumping through their own hoops (especially if they aren't yet tenured), consumed by their own research, or who are simply disengaged from the department completely. What this means is that you literally have to seek out a mentor; they will not come to you. The first thing you may want to look for is similar interest in terms of research. This should be something you look for when you are checking out the department to begin with, perhaps by asking questions during your initial visit or surfing the department's website for descriptions of professors' work, especially their research/publications. Obviously, if you can find a mentor with similar research interests there is a potential for joint publications. Not only will this allow you to get some publications on your vita, it may place your name next to someone who is well known in the area. However, an area of interest similar to your own does not make a good mentor in and of itself.

For women, finding a mentor can be harder than it is for men. While the majority of doctoral students are female, the majority of faculty are male (Wenniger and Conroy 2001; National Opinion Research Center 2009). This becomes important because women and men have different needs from mentors. As well, male and female faculty have different approaches to mentoring students. Men tend to mentor women differently than they do other men by sharing different advice and insider information (Kleiman 1980). Women's and men's socialization processes are different, and this creates some differences between men and women when it comes to mentoring (Kleiman 1980). Women, more than men, feel that we should *already* know an individual before approaching them for help, advice, or information (Kleiman 1980). We feel like we are using someone or manipulating them for our own ends if we don't have a preexisting relationship (Kleiman 1980). Female students may benefit from a mentor who can advise them academically as well as personally, e.g., on ways to balance family and emotions during graduate school. A female mentor might be better able to provide this kind of advice because of different socialization. On the other hand, a male mentor might be more inclined to involve a student in formal networking in the field. It is up to you to figure out what you need from a mentor, what styles different mentors have to offer (Kunselman et al. 2003), and how to put together a support team that can facilitate achievement of all of your objectives.

You may find, as we did, that there are no professors in your department with similar interests. This is not cause for panic – after all, if we had been determined to find a mentor who was interested in lesbian identity and state crime in China then we would still be looking today. There are mentors out there who will work with you despite differences, which is fine, because the primary purpose of finding a mentor is not to generate publications. The primary purpose of your mentor should be to make sure that you are making timely progress and that you are making the proper connections *outside* of your department. So, first and foremost, you want a mentor who is willing to dedicate some time and attention to you. One way to gauge a professor's willingness to work with you is to set up an appointment with the professor of interest and go with a list of questions. You should have a question or questions in each of the following areas:

- *Program of study.* Ask a random question about the program, such as "At what point should I form a committee for such and such?" If they don't know the answer off the top of their head, then they haven't been paying enough attention to the details that concern you. If they seem determined to help you find the answer, great; otherwise, run away as fast as you can.
- *Your area of interest.* Ask something about the topic of study you are currently focused on, such as where you might find sources. Remember, it doesn't matter if this is their area of interest or not; what matters is how willing they are to help you accomplish your goals. If the conversation about your area of interest somehow ends up back at their research agenda, run away as fast as you can.
- *Their work.* Ask the potential mentor about their interests. Oftentimes you will find that their interests go way beyond the short description you were given on line or when you visited the department. Not only will you learn about them, you may also discover that their interests do in fact connect to yours in some way.
- *Their job as mentor.* Ask them what they think their job (as it concerns graduate students) entails. If something along the lines of "helping them to develop successful careers" isn't on the list, or if something about their own research agenda is at the top of their list, run away as fast as you can.
- *The gestalt of who they are.* Find out who they are as a person, not just as an academic. Whoever becomes your mentor will be someone that you have

to spend a lot of time with, and there is nothing worse than working with someone who drives you crazy. Make sure that you actually like who they are and that you are compatible as a team. If you can't work well together, your relationship will ultimately be frustrating and fruitless. Think about it this way: if you were their equal, would you still work with them? If the answer is No, run away as fast as you can.

Unfortunately, it isn't always as easy as "setting up an appointment" because some professors, even those who might make good mentors, may not be in their office consistently. If this is the case, we suggest taking other routes to getting close to someone you think may be a good mentor. For example, when we wanted to get to know one of our mentors (who is quite often not in her office due to commuting) we signed up to be on a committee that she was chairing at the time and set up a meeting to "talk about our duties as members of the committee." What she thought was a routine meeting about committee business was actually an opportunity for us to begin building a relationship with her.

Seeking out mentors is key: while it would be nice if they came to us, especially considering that we are the ones paying for the degree, the fact of the matter is that this just doesn't happen as often as it should. You must take inventory of your department immediately upon entering the program – figure out who your potential mentors are and begin this foreshadowing interview process. The sooner you get a mentor, the better.

Having said this, it is also important to find more than one mentor. While it is necessary to find one person with whom you can work most closely, it is dangerous to put all of your eggs in one basket. While working on our own PhDs we watched seven professors leave our department. While one would hope that this is an out-of-the-ordinary number, as all departments lose faculty for some reason or another, and departmental attrition can mean losing your mentor at a crucial time in your program, it may have devastating consequences. Be sure to develop relationships with several people, and make sure that they are just as aware of your progress as your "primary" mentor is. Remember, when you go on the job market you need several references, and every one of them should be able to write your letter based on the knowledge they have gained by watching your progress over time. Having multiple mentors can only broaden your possibilities and strengthen your support system (Gray and Drew 2008). The more mentors that you have to go to, the more questions you will have answers to.

Not only should you have more than one mentor, you should have mentors in more than one place. This is where networking comes in, which can best be facilitated by your primary mentor. Of course, this requires attending conferences and the like where you actually have the opportunity to meet people from other universities. This means that if your mentor isn't encouraging you to go to conferences (especially the ones they are attending), then they aren't fulfilling one of their primary functions as your mentor. Conferences can introduce you to new mentors in several ways. The most obvious is through research sharing. Presenting your research may peak the interest of more accomplished scholars with similar interests, and can lead to publishing. Indeed, the first presentation that we gave as a duo resulted in our first coauthored publication – something that was largely accomplished through the networks that we formed while attending a conference. The truth is, though, that conferences are about more than just sharing ideas and growing the intellectual pool – there is a secret that only the best mentors will share with you.

The secret about conferences is that they're essentially big class reunions at which people are forced to share their work. While the sharing of new research is an integral part of knowledge production, it is not the only purpose of academic conferences. Undoubtedly your mentor is also attending in hopes of catching up with old friends, many of whom may be an asset to you. A good mentor will likely invite you to a function or two, and it is very important that you attend. Join in the conversations as much as possible (without monopolizing the discussion) and keep your ears open for links to your own interests. Always be prepared to give out your email address to others working in your area, because it is a surefire way to start relationships with people at different schools. This becomes very important once you're on the job market – if you've already worked (positively) with someone at the school where you're applying to, this person essentially becomes an additional reference. Moreover, these "outside" individuals may prove to be very useful mentors.

The truth is, though, that you cannot rely on casual conversation to get you very far in and of itself – the key is to get involved! Go to the conferences that are most relevant to your interests and find out how you can become an integral part of activities. Some annual meetings have "divisions," "sections," "committees," "subcommittees," events, meetings, and activities that are very welcoming to graduate students (such as the Division on Women and Crime of the American Society of Criminology, where this book was born). Without overextending yourself, get involved in these organizations and start making a name for yourself as early as possible. Doing so leads to almost instant reward – recognition by established scholars in national organizations, new relationships, research and publications. If you can involve yourself on a small scale during graduate school you will have already built a foundation to move quickly up the ranks in these organizations once you graduate – something you can use to your advantage in navigating future rites of passage (e.g., earning tenure and promotion).

Surviving the comprehensive exams

The problem with comprehensive exams is that they are different everywhere, and this is where your cohort and your mentor come in handy. Talk to everyone and anyone that has taken the exam before you begin, ask your mentor questions when you have them, and make sure you pour over any materials your department has available about the exam. Many graduate programs have created exam handbooks that you can request from your department chair or advisor, from the exam committee, or that you can find on the department web site. Although the format of exams (take-home versus in-house), content (broad versus specific knowledge), and depth (course content versus reading list you/ they have developed) varies by discipline and department (Mitchell 1996), there is some advice that can apply to any situation. Regardless of the particulars, you must know what you are getting into, anticipate the work load, and not die of exhaustion in the process.

First, know what you are getting yourself into. Don't wait until the last minute to find out the format, content, and depth of the exam. The minute you begin a program you should be finding out this important information. For most, exams are taken before you even begin working on a thesis or dissertation proposal, so plan ahead. While you want to give yourself enough time in the classroom first, you don't want to finish all of your coursework and then say, "Now, what about those exams?" Remember, the goal is to get *out* of graduate school successfully, not to spend ten years of your life there. Moreover, much of the reading and writing that you do in your classes can be applied to your exam. If you know what is expected on the exams ahead of time, you'll know if you should put any notes, papers, annotations, or books aside as you progress through your classes. For example, we both took an exam in criminology, and we knew that we would be tested extensively on our knowledge of theory and methods in this field. So, we created binders that were divided by theory (and then further divided by "camps" of theory) and methods (by types of methods or methods issues). Each time we read an article about a particular theory, methodological issue, or wrote a related paper, it was placed in the binder where it belonged. When it came time for the exam, all of our materials were gathered and in order. You don't want to find yourself looking for that "fantastic paper I wrote on feminist theory" a week before your comprehensive exam. Work smarter, not harder.

If you know what is expected of you on the exam, then you can anticipate the work load without panicking and, with any luck, keep your sanity and your life while you're at it. For most people, the toughest part of the exam is the additional reading that is required of you. Graduate students are already reading multiple books per week, so for most of us the thought of cramming in any more is a complete nightmare. The sooner you obtain the list before taking the exam, the longer you have to go through all of the material. Again, start early! Set weekly reading goals. Divide the number of books on the list by the number of weeks you have to prepare but add a few weeks (there will be weeks when you feel like you'll shoot yourself if you read one more book). You will need this to synthesize and possibly memorize information as well. Take brief notes on each book and (this is very important) write down page numbers, especially if your exam is going to be take-home. This will help recollection later on and you won't find yourself wondering on which of the 987 pages in that book was the fantastic quote about external validity?

Once you have mastered the reading and preparation, the only thing left to do is survive the test. This is easier said than done, but it is possible (you wouldn't have made it into grad school if it wasn't). How you survive the exam is specific to the format, so let's begin with take-home exams. There are a few things you should be doing in the week prior to the exam. First, prepare your family and friends. Tell them that you love them, but that you will be completely unavailable for the duration of the exam (and likely stressed out enough to scream at anyone who bothers you). Take care of anything that normally helps you procrastinate – clean the house, lock up the PlayStation, unplug the television, etc. Buy quick foods that can be heated up in the microwave, and stock the house full of snacks (this is a time when you definitely deserve junk food). Organize your work space – you should be done with all of your reading by this point, so gather *all* of the books from your list and arrange them in your office in some fashion that makes sense to you (e.g., by theoretical camp). Pull out the binder that you have been preparing and make a home for it right next to your computer, along with a fresh jump drive (because your paranoia will drive you to save your work every five minutes). Finally, make sure that all of your other work is done. If you have classes, be sure you are up to date on your work and tell your professors you will not be in attendance on the day or week of the exam. If you are teaching make sure that you have your lectures prepared or have arranged for a guest speaker, video, etc., and make sure that you have not assigned any work to be due on your exam day(s).

Much of the previous advice applies to the in-house exam as well, but you will want to spend the week before reviewing all of your notes because you likely will not be able to bring them with you. Be sure to focus on your weaknesses – if you know you aren't good with remembering names and dates, practice reciting them without looking at your notes. Whether you are taking the exam in-house or at home, be sure to give yourself some time the morning you begin it. Get a good night's sleep and eat a healthy breakfast (or an unhealthy breakfast – this is a day to do whatever makes you happy).

When you finally face the questions, don't panic. Take a few minutes to read them carefully, and begin by answering the hard stuff. If you are in-house, jot down the things you know you struggle with, like names and dates, because you will have forgotten them by the time the afternoon rolls around. You may want to jot out major materials you want to be sure to include and/or even outline your response(s). Plan your time. If you have three questions, for example, and twelve hours to take the exam, spend three hours on each question and then spend the last three hours revisiting and fixing your answers. If you have five days, spend a day on each of the questions and two days editing, adding, deleting, and rearranging.

It is unlikely that you will have one straightforward question. Most exams have multiple parts (e.g., theory, methods, etc.) and, as you become accustomed to in graduate school, most individual questions have multiple parts themselves. Be sure to answer *all* parts of the question(s) – if you fail to do so, the evaluators will think that you didn't know the complete answer, even if you simply forgot to mention something. On the other hand, do *not* answer a question that is not there. In academia you are trained to be longwinded, but the comprehensive exam is not the place to practice it. Trying to be grandiose in your writing often leads to pointless diatribes that stray from the subject at hand. If you are asked to answer a question about protecting research participants, and you go off on a tangent about the significance of ethnographic studies, you have just wasted your time and suggested to the evaluators that you don't know enough about human subject protection to write an essay about it. Stay focused and continuously remind yourself that you've gotten this far, so you *can* do this.

Regardless of how prepared you are, the answers that you develop on the comprehensive exams may not be your best work. General Patton may have said that diamonds are made from pressure, but for most of us pressure just promotes gibberish (especially if we are forced to write something in eight hours with no resources at our disposal). Most faculty members recognize this, because, after all, they had to take some of these stupid things, too. This is precisely why most programs couple your exam with an oral defense. If this is the case for you, reread the questions and answers, and take notes if you missed something. The defense is designed for you to fill in the gaps, so take the opportunity to prove to the faculty that you know what you're talking about. Bring a copy of the questions, your answers, and any other materials you might want (like your binder) to the defense (if materials are allowed at your oral). These meetings can feel like an interrogation, but there is no need to be intimidated or defensive. Answer all questions calmly and completely, and don't be afraid to pause and think when you need to – it is not a bad characteristic to be reflective. Once the entire exam and defense are successfully completed, party like a rock star.

Surviving the thesis or dissertation

First and foremost, remember that your dissertation (and certainly your thesis) is *not* your opus magnum (Gray and Drew 2008). We repeat: it is *not* your opus magnum. This is *not* to say that you should not strive to make it an amazing piece of work that you can be proud of. This *is* to say that your ultimate goal is to get *out* of graduate school, not spend the rest of your life there (Gray and Drew 2008). Unless you are Emile Durkheim a dissertation cannot catapult you into academic stardom, so don't fool yourself into thinking it will. For most, a good thesis will earn you a pat on the back from your mentor and free drinks from your friends. A good dissertation will give you a few articles or, at most, a book. This is not even enough to earn your tenure at most institutions, so don't spend three years writing something that will only help you survive the first year or so of a real job. Nevertheless, it will be the longest thing you have written up until this point in your life, so it requires an immense amount of time and planning.

Generally, the actual research and writing of a thesis will take about a semester, while it will take about a year for the dissertation. This time frame, however, doesn't include the planning stages. Before beginning your project you need to form a committee, conceptualize your work, and set a timeline for yourself. Forming an appropriate committee is key to your success (Bolker 1998; Mitchell 1996), and for each member you add you should ask yourself three questions. What kind of relationship do I have with this person? What is their area of interest and expertise? And, most important, what is their "committee" reputation? In most cases, putting your primary mentor on your committee (usually as the chair) is ideal, as you should already have a good working relationship with them. It probably goes without saying, but don't choose a professor who tore your final paper apart when you took their class – if they didn't like a twenty-five-page paper that you wrote, how do think they will feel about something that is hundreds of pages long? Remember, your goal is to finish your degree, not to become a professional student.

It is great if your committee (or someone on it) is an expert on the topic you have chosen. However, it isn't completely necessary. What *is* necessary is a committee of people dedicated to helping *you* become an expert on that topic. So long as the people you are working with are willing to step outside of the box, you are good to go. With one exception, that is. If you have chosen to conduct a study on topic X and your department just happens to have one of the leading scholars in topic X, it is not a good idea to form a committee without that person. Prospective employers see your thesis/dissertation title on your vita and will recognize that you chose not to include an expert that was at your disposal; hence they will question your scholarliness or collegiality or both. If you absolutely cannot work with the expert for some reason you should consider changing your topic or, at the very least, finding another expert of equal caliber from perhaps outside your department.

The last question (i.e., what is their "committee" reputation?) is probably the most important, especially when it comes to finishing your degree in a timely manner. This is when you should be talking to other students and taking a look at the person's history. Did other students have positive experiences working with them, or have they earned the reputation of being a nightmare? It is often a good sign if the person has been chosen for many committees, but you also want to be sure that they are not overextended – you need as much attention as you can get. Find out how long it took the last few students who worked with them to finish their thesis or dissertation. If they all took longer than you would like, you probably should not consider adding the person to your committee. It's quite possible that they took so long because the person has unrealistic expectations, something that you cannot afford.

You should begin conceptualizing your work very early on in your program. If you have an idea of which direction you are headed, then you can gather books, articles, and other materials as you come across them, which saves you a lot of time later on. As with the comprehensive exam, create some sort of filing system that complements the scope of your project. Begin your proposal one or two semesters before you want to have your project approved. Organize your proposal to your advantage to what degree you can. You are going to have to submit a proposal to an institutional review board (IRB) in addition to your committee, so you may be able to format your proposal according to IRB standards. Ultimately, your committee wants to see the same information as the IRB, so "double dip" to the extent that you can. Be thorough in your proposal, especially in the literature review and method sections – not only will this make your plan clearer to those who review it (reducing the chance of major revisions), but you will also have well-developed or maybe even nearly complete chapters for the actual thesis or dissertation (Mauch and Birch 1998).

Be realistic. Academics are often hopeless romantics, and many of us want to embark on earth-shattering studies that will change the course of humanity. This is fine – except when that study is your thesis or dissertation. Certainly you want to produce meaningful, original work (which is, of course, the point), but you need to be cognizant of your resources and your time. This is not the point in your career when you should decide to conduct interviews of 400 people if you cannot afford a transcriber who charges $20 an hour. Most important, be flexible – there is no shame in setting a goal of 100 hours of ethnographic observation and cutting it down to fifty when you realize that you produce ten pages of field notes for every one hour of observation. So long as your department requirements, committee, and the IRB agree to the changes you make there is no harm in recognizing your limitations – especially if it means finishing your degree in a timely manner.

Finally, just as with the comprehensive exam, set goals (Mauch and Birch 1998). The moment you defend your proposal, discuss a final defense date with your committee. Doing this will help you avoid falling into the black hole that many graduate students find themselves in once they are ABD (All But Dissertation). When we are taking classes it is easy to take for granted the fact that our professors set due dates for us – these keep us on track and force us to finish things in a timely manner. The freedom of a thesis or dissertation is academic suicide for some – you find yourself avoiding campus (because you have no mandated reason to be there) and suddenly all of the things that help you procrastinate are amplified. This is precisely why self-discipline is of the utmost importance. Without it, you will become that person whom professors and other grad students talk about in quiet whispers – you know, that person who has been "ABD" for ten years that no one has ever laid eyes on. Moreover, when you finally do reach the job market, prospective employers are going to wonder why you couldn't seem to pull yourself together. Why would anyone want a colleague who can't manage completing one project?

Just as when you divided the number of books by weeks for the comprehensive exam, divide the number of months by the number of chapters you intend to write. (See Mauch and Birch 1998 for a timeline checklist.) Again, add a few months or weeks for good measure, as there will be times when the thought of writing one more sentence will send you into convulsions. However, you should also avoid taking too much advantage of breaks in your work. Holiday or spring break or summer might seem like good time to take off, but these breaks can really add up and disrupt your whole process. Leaving your data for too long can put you further back than you might expect. Draw up a calendar of deadlines and give a copy to your committee chair for the sake of accountability. You will find it a lot harder to put things off if you have made a commitment to another person. Beyond that, it will give your chair the impression that you mean business (which will motivate them) and it will also allow them to anticipate when they need to set aside time to read your work.

Prior to the defense you should sit down with your chair and ask them how they like to conduct defenses, what departmental norms and routines there are. Departments, chairs, and committee members conduct defenses in different manners, and you want to know what to expect – to the degree that they will tell you. Ask if you will get the chance to present your work prior to questioning, and find out how long you will have. Create an outline of your presentation, and practice in front of friends or family. Keep in mind that your committee has already read your paper, so there is no need to regurgitate the entire thing. Use the opportunity to highlight what you feel is the most important contribution of your work. Like your comprehensive exam defense, don't be intimidated or defensive. Remember that you are the expert on the topic and remind yourself that you *can* do this – after all, you did pass all of your classes and exams. Don't hesitate to pause and reflect when you are stumped, and be honest. If your committee throws you for a loop by asking some question from out in left field, simply admit that you hadn't thought of that before and share your current thoughts. Sometimes the defense is not always about what you have already done but about what you can do on the spot or what you might do with the work in the future. Once the defense is successfully completed, party like a rock star. You have finally made it to academic stardom. Well ... almost.

The next step

So you have finally jumped through the hoops and survived the rites of passage that define graduate school. The good news is that you can finally sit on the other side of the table. Instead of defending your work to others, people will now defend their work to you. The bad news is, graduate school is only the beginning of an ever-changing journey. Even though it feels like you have survived the apocalypse, graduate school is like the first 100 miles of a 1,000 mile road trip. You wouldn't have come this far if you weren't up to a challenge, so put on your seat belt and start your engines. Now it is time to put all of your hard work to good use ... it is time to get a "real" job.

References

Bauman, K. J., and Graf, N. L. (2003) *Educational Attainment, 2000,*Washington, DC: U.S. Census Bureau.

Bolker, J. (1998) *Writing your Dissertation in Fifteen Minutes a Day*, New York: Holt.

Gray, P., and Drew, D. E. (2008) "What they didn't teach you in graduate school," *Chronicle of Higher Education.* Online. Available: < http://chronicle.com/article/What-They-Didnt-Teach-You-/4393/> (accessed June 4, 2009).

Kleiman, C. (1980) *Women's Networks: The Complete Guide to Getting a Better Job, Advancing your Career, and Feeling Great as a Woman through Networking*, New York: Lippincott & Crowell.

Kunselman, J., Hensley, C., and Tewksbury, R. (2003) "Mentoring in academe: Models for facilitating academic development," *Journal of Criminal Justice Education*, 14 (1): 17–35.

Marshall, S., and Green, N. (2004) *Your Ph.D. Companion*, Oxford: How-to Books.

Mauch, J. E., and Birch, J. W. (1998) *Guide to the Successful Thesis and Dissertation: A Handbook for Students and Faculty*, New York: Dekker.

Mitchell, L. (1996) *The Ultimate Grad School Survival Guide*, Princeton, NJ: Petersons.

National Opinion Research Center (2009) *Survey of Earned Doctorates Fact Sheet*. Online. Available: <http://www.norc.uchicago.edu/NR/rdonlyres/B40E56EC-9A4F-4892-B871-E330BB689CD9/0/SEDFFactSheet.pdf> (accessed August 23, 2009).

Rossman, M. H. (2002) *Negotiating Graduate School: A Guide for Students*, 2nd edn, Thousand Oaks, CA: Sage.

Wenniger, M. D., and Conroy, M. H. (2001) *Gender, Equity or Bust! On the Road to Campus Leadership with Women in Higher Education*, San Francisco, CA: Jossey-Bass.

2 Strategies for success on the job market

Kate Luther and Nancy A. Wonders

A pivotal rite of passage for those pursuing academic careers is to successfully obtain a job! For those who are still graduate students, there will be a temptation to put this chapter aside based on the incorrect assumption that the job preparation process begins late in a student's graduate career. Instead, we urge readers to devote careful attention to this chapter very early in their graduate studies since preparation for the job market actually begins the moment the decision is made to enter graduate school. In this chapter, we provide useful information that will help you to strategically prepare for the job of your dreams. Based on our experience as job seekers and as members of many search committees, we offer tips on living life as a job candidate, when and where to search for positions, what items to include in your application materials, how to prepare for the interview process, and suggested ways to distinguish yourself during the job search.

Living life as a job candidate

It is important to start thinking about yourself as a potential job candidate from the very beginning of graduate school. In this section, we propose a number of strategies that will help to ensure you are well informed about the demands associated with obtaining an academic job and that your graduate school experiences position you to be an excellent candidate for the job you desire.

Take advantage of opportunities

First and foremost, take advantage of opportunities designed to inform you about the job search process and the academic job market. While this sounds like an obvious suggestion, you'd be amazed by how many graduate students do not take advantage of workshops and professional development opportunities that could make them informed and distinctive job applicants. While institutions differ in the opportunities they provide, many offer workshops about the job search process that help graduate students early on. These workshops are typically attended by those who expect to obtain a job immediately, despite the fact that the information provided is frequently most beneficial to those early in their graduate careers. Learning that a particular area of expertise is "hot" is only beneficial to those who still have time to develop that expertise. Similarly, learning that it is better to teach a variety of courses, rather than just one, is going to be most helpful to those who can still adjust their teaching schedule to evidence their instructional breadth. Although you may only have a few teaching and research experiences to list on your curriculum vitae (CV) right now, attending a workshop on how to prepare a CV will allow you to anticipate what information to keep track of and what an outstanding CV should eventually contain.

Sessions on the job search are also commonplace at many scholarly meetings and provide exceptionally valuable information about the current and anticipated job markets that can shape decisions you make now. Check professional conference programs for sessions pertaining to the interview process, careers in your field, and preparation for the job search. And, remember that it is never too early to start attending these sessions.

We also recommend that graduate students take advantage of opportunities to participate in faculty search processes and to attend job talks at their university. At many universities, graduate students play an active role in the search process, even serving on search committees. Typically, a great deal can be learned by listening to the kinds of questions asked of potential candidates. After attending a few job talks, it will become obvious there are some common questions that are asked of most candidates regarding their research and teaching. By attending job talks it is also possible to observe diverse presentation styles and consider the demeanor of various candidates. It is important to pay attention to both those approaches that impress the hiring committee and the department – and those that offend the hiring committee and the department. The experience of observing job talks, taking candidates to lunch, and hearing deliberations within the search committee (if permitted) can provide valuable information about what the interview process looks like, as well as about which candidates are most likely be most successful.

Another way to prepare for the job market is to talk with new faculty members at your university and in your personal and professional networks about their job search experiences. As recent candidates they will surely have a great deal of practical advice to offer about what they could have done early in their graduate careers to be better prepared for the job search process.

Develop a clear sense of your dream position

In order to obtain the ideal job at the end of graduate school, it is helpful to begin to develop a clear sense of your dream position early on in your graduate career. Different academic contexts are linked to differing expectations regarding the mix of teaching, research, and service that is required. If you are able to clarify the kind of setting you would like to have as your academic home, you can begin early to cultivate the skills, expertise, and credentials required to make you both a strong candidate and a successful faculty member in that setting.

Would you like to be at a state university with a diverse student body, at an institution with a strong research mission, at a private liberal arts college, or at a community college serving working adults? There are many different kinds of academic settings and each offers unique benefits and challenges. For example, universities with a very strong research mission typically seek individuals with an excellent record of publication and external funding, and also expect high research productivity from all faculty members throughout the duration of their careers. At the same time, the undergraduate teaching and advising load will typically be much lighter than at other types of institutions. For those who love research, this may be a perfect fit. However, for those who love teaching and research equally, it might be ideal to seek employment at a medium-size state university where there is typically greater balance between the emphasis on research and teaching. And for those who are clear that their passion is exclusively teaching, it is possible that their "dream position" will be found at a private liberal arts college, where a focus on teaching, mentoring, and student support is prioritized.

Deciding what kind of academic work environment is best for you is a complex task. You will need to consider quite a few things, such as:

- Is research the most important priority in my academic life?
- Do I want to teach and mentor undergraduate students or graduate students?
- What balance of scholarship, teaching, and service do I want to have in my future position?

To begin to understand the differing expectations that accompany various academic settings, start talking with faculty who work at different kinds of colleges and universities. Because professional conferences attract participants from a wide range of academic contexts, they offer a rich opportunity to explore what kind of position is right for you. At the next scholarly meeting you attend, ask the person sitting next to you at a session where they work. Tell them you are a graduate student and you'll be on the job market in the future. Ask them about the requirements for teaching, scholarship, and service and how they feel about that mix. You might also ask these questions of faculty at your own institution. Ask them about how they came to the university and what elements factored into their decision making. Additionally, use your research skills to observe the environment of your university. Would you want to be a new faculty member at a university like this? Do you think you would be happy with the work–life balance of new faculty members? How do you feel about the expectations for publication, research, teaching, and service?

We cannot stress enough how important it is for you to start figuring out what kind of university or college you want to call home. Once you develop an idea about your dream position, you can begin to prepare to be the ideal candidate for that job. If you plan to seek employment at a research university, take advantage of every grant writing, methods, and statistics workshop your university or department offers. Become a regular at one or more professional associations by presenting papers, organizing sessions, and participating in specialty divisions. This networking will help to ensure that your research – and you – are known beyond your institution. Get involved in large-scale research projects in your department. Make sure that by the end of your graduate school career you have done everything possible to make yourself an excellent candidate for a research-intensive job. On the other hand, if you know you want to be at a university that prioritizes teaching, start preparing yourself to be a good "teacher-scholar." Participate in teaching and pedagogy workshops and take advantage of opportunities to have your teaching evaluated. When attending scholarly meetings, make sure to attend teaching workshops and other sessions focused on connecting your scholarship to your teaching. By knowing what kind of position you want you can begin immediately to prepare to be an excellent candidate for your dream position.

Always interviewing

Remember you are *always* interviewing for a job. What we mean by this is that the "interview" actually starts well before you apply for a job. Presentations at conferences, interaction with other scholars at professional meetings, and work you perform within your department all provide important information about you that will profoundly influence your job prospects. The way you present yourself throughout graduate school will have a significant impact on your subsequent success on the job market. For instance, let's say you give a presentation at a scholarly meeting and a tenured faculty member stays afterward to talk with you about your work. This conversation goes well and the faculty member is completely impressed with your scholarship and professionalism, as well as with your presentation style. Two years later, long after you've forgotten about this conversation, you end up sending an application to the very university where this faculty member works. As the faculty member is reviewing applicant files, she comes across your name and remembers your engaging conversation. When she and other faculty members meet to discuss their shortlist, she is able to tell the department about how much you impressed her and to strongly recommend you be invited for an interview.

This vignette provides a window into the complex way your everyday interactions shape the likelihood you will obtain your dream job later on. This is not to say that every conversation at a scholarly meeting will result in an offer of employment, but it is to say that your personal style and professional interactions during graduate school do matter. The academic world is a very small place. There are a limited number of scholars in each field and a limited number of new PhDs each year. The impression you make, whether positive or negative, may leave a lasting mark. Thus, when you are socializing at the conference hotel bar, giving a presentation, or casually meeting your mentor's colleagues, remember it is all part of the interview process.

The job search

In this section, we provide information about the job search process, including when and where to search for a position, how to interpret job postings, and how to prepare application materials.

Where and when to search

As you get close to finishing graduate school, it is time to start looking for academic positions. The first question you may ask is – Where do I begin to look for jobs? There are a variety of places to find postings for academic jobs. One of the easiest places to start is *The Chronicle of Higher Education*, where they offer an online job database that you can search by discipline. Likewise, most major professional associations in your field now have an online job bank that you can search if you are a member, and reasonable student membership rates are common. For instance, the American Sociological Association has a job bank that is available to all of its members. Another related place to look for jobs is in discipline-specific newsletters. For example, *The Criminologist*, a publication of the American Society of Criminology, regularly publishes job listings. Some professional associations even conduct preliminary interviews at their annual conference. This can be an excellent way to learn more about available positions and to begin to practice and develop strong interviewing skills. Should you decide to participate in these preliminary interviews, be sure to read carefully the section "Interviewing" later in this chapter, since advance preparation will help you to distinguish yourself during this process.

It is also possible to search for job announcements on the human resource websites of select universities. While this approach can be time-consuming, it is especially valuable if you are restricted to applying for jobs in a particular geographical area or have an interest in particular universities.

A question closely related to "where to look" is "When should I start looking for a job?" The answer to this question really depends upon you and your situation. In an ideal world, it would be great to become ABD (All But Dissertation) in the academic year before you apply for a job. Then at the end of the summer, after you've made significant progress on your dissertation, you could start looking at jobs for the following academic year. You'd be ready to meet all of the early fall application deadlines and your dissertation would be close to completion by the time you were invited for campus interviews in the late fall or early winter. But, as we all know (and many of you are starting to figure out), graduate school does not always proceed as we hoped it would. Some of you will know by July that you'll be defending your dissertation in December and filing it by May. Others, though, will have a less definite plan.

You may know that you could complete your dissertation within the school year, but that you'd like one more year to finish it.

Whatever your "plan of attack" is, here are a few general tips regarding when to apply and the typical timeline for applications and interviews. First, the earliest job announcements are posted in the late summer. While some announcements will not be publicized until December or later, for most disciplines the majority of ads will appear in the fall. Second, the first due dates for applications are in mid-September. A typical job candidate will have a few applications that are due in September, but most of them will be due between October and December. Third, just like varying due dates for applications, there is much variation in interview timelines. For those positions with applications due in September, if all goes as planned in the department and at the university, interviews with candidates will typically take place in November. Other universities with later deadlines might not bring candidates out until January or February. Be prepared for the job hunt to take the better part of your last year of graduate school. Even if you apply to universities with application deadlines in September, you may not get an interview until January or February.

What to consider as you're looking at job postings

As you start looking at job postings you'll notice each posting provides similar information. Job postings typically start by listing the university (the department and the contact person for the job), the position and rank (instructor, assistant, associate, or full professor), and the salary range. After this initial information, there is often a detailed description of the position. In this section, you'll want to pay close attention to a few things:

- Is it a tenure track or visiting position?
- Is there a limited term of appointment for this position?
- What areas of research and teaching expertise are desired?
- Is the funding certain or is the position "contingent upon funding?"
- Do you need to have your dissertation completed by the start date?

It is imperative to familiarize yourself with the position before you decide to apply. There are two reasons for this. First, it is a poor use of your time to apply for a job for which you do not meet the qualifications. If you are on the job market while also working on a dissertation, it is very important to be aware that the application process can be very time-consuming. Be selective and apply for jobs that are a good fit with your qualifications so you do not misuse time that could be spent completing your dissertation. Second, it is a waste of time for the hiring committee to read an application from an applicant who is clearly not qualified for a position. In the interest of everyone's time, make sure to take a few minutes and read over the job postings before you decide to apply.

As mentioned before, it is essential to know what *you* want in a future position. In reviewing job advertisements, it is wise to prioritize applying for positions that you would actually consider taking. Because job advertisements are typically very brief, it can be incredibly valuable to obtain additional information regarding the position. The school's departmental and university websites will typically contain a great deal of information that may help potential applicants to better assess the nature of the position and whether it is a good fit with their expertise and interests. For example, even a quick glance at the posted curriculum should help to determine whether your expertise would complement or expand the existing course offerings. A review of faculty research should help you to assess whether you can expect to have research colleagues and if your research focus is consistent with existing departmental specializations. Remember also that you should feel free to contact the chair of the search committee to learn more about a particular position. We know of more than one individual who did not initially apply for a position, but then was persuaded to do so by a member of the search committee who provided new information about a particular position and/or location. One person we know had rejected the idea of living in Arizona, assuming that all of the universities there were in a hot, dry desert climate; when the search committee chair described the beautiful four-season mountain environment in which this particular university was located, this individual decided to apply – and in doing so secured her dream job!

We encourage you to also consider quality of life issues as you weigh whether a particular position is right for you but, as the story above suggests, be sure your judgments are based in fact. Are you comfortable living in an urban area or do you want to live in a more suburban or rural college town? Do you need to be in a specific location to conduct your research (e.g., near a prison for correctional research, near an urban center for urban ethnography)? Is public transportation and/or access to the outdoors important to you? While many graduate students cannot imagine being picky about the location of their future job because they are primarily focused on just *getting* a job, it is wise to consider whether the location fits your lifestyle and whether you are willing to adapt to a new location. Of course, if you are partnered, you will also want to consider the needs of the other person in the relationship. Some questions to think about include: Can your partner move anywhere or is s/he limited to a particular locale/region due to work or family obligations? If you are a dual academic couple, are you willing to work at two different institutions in the same city/region? And, if you have children, is this an area where you can comfortably raise a family? Some institutions do have partner accommodation programs. If such a program exists, it will typically be described on the university's human resources or personnel department website.

It may seem premature to consider these questions *before* applying for a job, but if you wish to have a position that is a good fit with your professional and personal goals it is important to prioritize applying for those positions that have the highest likelihood of ensuring you will enjoy a successful and happy life.

The application

Now that you have narrowed down the list of potentially desirable positions, it is time to tackle the application process. We suggest you create a chart that will allow you to keep track of application details and due dates for each position. Begin with applications that have the earliest due dates. It is safe to assume that an application due date of September 15th means that *all* materials (including your letters of recommendation) must have arrived by the 15th. In addition to listing due dates, make a list of all of the materials that are required for each application, and list key contact information. Requirements for each application will vary, but here is a list of common requirements:

- A cover letter.
- A curriculum vitae.
- A research statement and samples of scholarly work.
- A teaching portfolio, including a statement of teaching philosophy, sample course syllabi, and teaching evaluations.
- Letters of recommendation.
- Official university transcripts.

It is important to be aware that search committees may be required to only consider materials that were explicitly solicited in their ad; as a result, if you decide to send supplemental materials, be sure to also briefly characterize these items in your cover letter.

A few tips regarding the application process may be helpful. It is extremely important to spend significant time working on the cover letter and CV, since these are the first – and most important – documents considered by hiring committees. If these two documents do not meet the minimum criteria *and* stand out, your application will be disregarded.

Consider the cover letter as your first introduction to the hiring committee. The cover letter creates a "first impression" and shapes the way the hiring committee examines the rest of your materials. The cover letter must be well written, clearly organized, and grammatically perfect, and it *must* speak directly to the job advertisement. If the job description calls for someone with well-established credentials in teaching, outline your teaching experience. If a willingness to teach methods is requested, be sure to state whether you are willing to develop and teach this course. If a clear research agenda is required, describe your current and planned research agenda in detail. Do not expect a committee to conduct an archeological dig on your CV to figure out if you are a good fit with the posted ad; instead, it is your job to write a cover letter that convinces them you are perfect for the posted job.

While cover letters will vary depending on your discipline and the type of position for which you are applying, there is some information that is typically included in a cover letter. The letter should address: the name of the position (there may be multiple searches underway), a brief summary of your credentials that make it evident that you meet – and hopefully exceed – minimum qualifications for the position, a clear statement regarding expected completion of the PhD and evidence of your progress (e.g., including very specific information regarding degree progress, as well as anticipated defense and graduation dates), a statement regarding the fit between your research and teaching expertise and this particular position, your interest in this position/and this institution, and your future research and teaching plans. The depth of attention to future research and teaching should depend upon the type of university to which you are applying. It is important to provide specific details and examples that allow your cover letter to stand out from the rest. For example, if you write that you love connecting your research to your teaching, provide a specific example of how you do this in your classes. After the first 100, most cover letters start to sound the same to the hiring committee. Make sure to include details in your cover letter that help the committee to remember it – and you.

It is important for your cover letter to highlight and complement your CV. In your cover letter, your goal is to draw attention to key accomplishments and to convince the hiring committee that you would be the ideal candidate for the position. The CV provides detailed information about all of your accomplishments. A typical graduate student CV should include information about:

- *Education.* Include all degrees received. (If you are a "PhD candidate," provide the date you expect to complete your degree.)
- *Professional employment.* List previous academic, research, and professional positions held – indicate the title of the position, the location, dates, and a brief description of the type of work/project.
- *Scholarship/research.* List all publications (create separate headings for those under review or in preparation), grants (submitted and/or obtained), conference papers and/or presentations, and professional development related to research.
- *Teaching.* List teaching experience (be sure to provide information about your level of responsibility for courses in which you were a TA), teaching interests (ideally, these should be consistent with the posted ad), and professional development experiences related to teaching.
- *Honors and awards.* Note any award or recognition you have received from your department, university, or professional organizations.
- *Professional activities.* List sessions you have chaired or organized at conferences, leadership roles in professional organizations or within your university/department; work on behalf of journals or publishers; significant community service.
- *Professional affiliations.* List professional organizations to which you belong.

- *References*. List complete contact information for at least three professional references. (If you are ABD or have just graduated, include your dissertation chair.)

It is essential to be honest and straightforward in the presentation of these items. While misleading information on a CV may get you an interview, it will almost certainly cause you to lose the job offer once your deception is discovered – and it will be, since the academic community is actually remarkably small.

We strongly recommend you draft a general template of your cover letter and CV, but that you put time into customizing both documents for each individual position. It is important to organize your CV so that it features your strongest qualifications for each particular position. For instance, if you are applying to a Research I university, scholarship and publications should appear early in your CV. In contrast, if you're applying to a teaching-oriented university, your teaching experience should appear earlier. As you are reviewing your CV, make sure it is well organized, easy to read (be careful to avoid using too many fonts), and that your expertise clearly fits the job description.

In order to heighten the likelihood of receiving an interview, you should expect to devote some quality time to preparing these materials. It is extremely important to edit your CV and cover letter. While this seems obvious, you would be surprised how many applications contain mistakes and incomplete information – or are addressed to the wrong university! We strongly recommend you share your materials with peers and mentors and ask for their careful review. Consider hiring a professional editor to ensure that the materials are perfect. You only have one shot at impressing the hiring committee.

It is wise to conduct careful research on the universities and departments to which you plan to apply so that you can gain an understanding of what is valued at that institution. For instance, if a university's mission statement focuses on service to the wider community, it would be very smart to incorporate some commentary about service into your cover letter. If the department has a strong international focus, it is in your interest to comment on your fit with this priority.

One of the most common reasons applications are late is because of delayed letters of recommendation. While you cannot ensure your letter writers will file them promptly, there are some things that can increase the likelihood that letters of recommendation arrive on time. Ask recommenders to prepare a template letter on your behalf far in advance of the due date. Ideally, a draft letter could be prepared a month or more before your application is due. Once individuals have agreed to write a letter on your behalf, provide them with drafts of the materials you will include in your application (e.g., cover letter and CV) and the actual job advertisement. Additionally, while it isn't recommended that you pester letter writers, we do suggest you check in with them and provide them with a friendly reminder of the upcoming application due date if you want to increase the likelihood that reference letters will arrive on time.

Interviews and campus visits

If your application makes it on to the shortlist, you will be contacted to schedule either a telephone interview and/or a campus interview. In this section, we describe what to expect during these interviews and offer a few suggestions that will help you excel during the interview process.

The phone interview

A great many institutions utilize phone interviews to further narrow the pool of acceptable candidates. If you are contacted for a phone interview, it is a sure sign you have made it to the shortlist and that the search committee is very interested in you. If you receive a call to schedule a phone interview, be enthusiastic on the phone and try to be flexible in scheduling the interview; however, we do not recommend you agree to a phone interview on the spot unless you are already very familiar with the department. The reason to give yourself a day or so to prepare is because the most important thing you can do to distinguish yourself during the phone interview is to spend significant time familiarizing yourself with the department and university – a point we have already emphasized throughout this chapter. It is incredibly impressive to interact with a candidate who is prepared to engage the university's mission, the undergraduate and graduate curriculum, faculty publications, and key areas of departmental specialization. Your goal is to be that candidate!

During the telephone interview, be aware that the search committee has a limited amount of time, so longwinded answers can be a problem. Ask at the outset how long the interview will be so you are aware of time constraints. Be sure to elaborate upon each answer, but also keep your answers well organized and to the point. A candidate who can't stop talking is just as problematic as one who gives only Yes or No answers. Telephone interviewing is a bit of an art, so your interview will be strengthened if you practice a telephone interview in advance of the real thing. Be sure to prepare a few questions to ask of the search committee to establish your genuine interest in the position, the university, and the surrounding community. If your phone interview goes well, you will then be invited for a campus interview.

Preparing for the campus interview

If you are invited for an on-campus interview, there are several ways you can prepare to ensure that your interview will be a success. First, talk with people who have served on hiring committees. Spend some time discussing the interview process and what impressed and did not impress them about previous job candidates. Also speak with other graduate students who have been successful on the job market (e.g., look up some past graduate students and send them an email or give them a call). It is extremely valuable to talk with others who have had recent success on the job market.

Once you've spent some time familiarizing yourself with the interview process, you'll want to make some specific preparations for the interview. One of the most important things to prepare for is the questions you'll be asked at the interview. Interestingly enough, most hiring committees ask similar questions. Some typical questions include:

- How does your research contribute to the discipline?
- What theories and methods do you employ in your research?
- What courses do you wish to teach now – and in the future?
- What contributions would you make to our teaching/research mission?

It can be very valuable to anticipate these questions and to practice your answers in advance.

Additionally, there is one important thing for you to remember as you prepare for your campus visit – if a university is inviting you to campus, they *want* you. The interview is an opportunity for the search committee to assess your qualifications and fit with the department, but it is also a chance for you to determine whether the position is a good one for *you*. They are interviewing you but, just as important, you are interviewing them.

Preparing for individual meetings

We wish to emphasize again the value of conducting advance research on the faculty in the department and on the hiring committee, as well as on the university, city, and state. This research will help you prepare questions for individual meetings and to evidence your interest in the faculty and their work, as well as in the surrounding university and local community. Nothing is worse than meeting with a job candidate who appears to be only interested in talking about him/herself. A candidate who is not interested in the research and teaching expertise of individual faculty demonstrates lack of interest in the department. Prior to your visit, research the publication history of faculty and read some recent work so that you can engage in meaningful conversation with each faculty member. This research will also help you understand the theoretical and methodological orientation of various faculty members so you can better field their questions during your research presentation.

We encourage you to request meetings with a few individuals outside of the department. You might ask to meet with the head of research or professional development, the director of women's studies, or a faculty member in another department. Such individuals can help you to understand how the department is viewed within the context of the broader university environment. We also advise you to meet with students, particularly if the department has a graduate program, since they can provide a unique perspective on the department. It is wise to meet with a realtor, as well, to ensure that you have an accurate idea regarding the cost of living. If you have children, it is ideal to visit a school or two so that you have a firsthand impression about educational options.

It is essential to realize that everyone with whom you have contact during the interview is important. We know of candidates who were eliminated from consideration because of the way they treated staff and students, believing they were not important enough to treat with interest and respect. Remember that most faculty members remain at an institution a long time, so the search committee will be paying careful attention to every aspect of your behavior. The hiring committee is not just looking at you as a scholar, but also as a future colleague. Thus, during the informal parts of the interview (e.g., over coffee, at dinner, or over drinks), make sure to present yourself as someone they'd like to have in their department. The perfect candidate is a strong researcher and/or teacher *and* a nice person!

Preparing for the research talk

Almost all interviews require some kind of research presentation. The research talk is one of the most important aspects of the interview and frequently makes the difference between who receives the job offer and who does not.

It is essential to prepare a tightly organized job talk with a well-crafted introduction, an overview of central theoretical and methodological approaches, several key substantive points and research findings, and a strong conclusion. Use your best teaching skills during the presentation (this is especially important if you will not be giving a separate teaching presentation). Be comfortable, engaging, make eye contact, use visuals for support, and leave plenty of time to field questions and encourage discussion. Lively discussion, even if it is contentious, is a sure sign that you have engaged your audience and that your work has been thought provoking!

If you are currently a graduate student, you will typically be expected to present your dissertation research; your presentation should show substantial progress toward completion of that project by reporting on preliminary findings and tentative conclusions. It is very useful to bring a brief one-page summary of your research presentation that can be provided to faculty members in attendance and to those who are unable to attend your talk.

Preparing for the class lecture

In addition to preparing for a research presentation, you may need to prepare an in-class teaching demonstration. Universities that prioritize teaching often want to make sure you are a strong, knowledgeable, and dynamic teacher. Universities take different approaches when setting up teaching demonstrations; some universities expect candidates to lecture on an assigned topic, while other universities may ask job candidates to use diverse teaching techniques to address a topic in the applicant's specialty area. While there is no single correct way to teach a class during an interview, we'd like to share some ideas that have worked well in the past.

- In advance of your presentation, ask if you can speak with the regular instructor of the class to learn more about the students, the classroom atmosphere, and the topics covered thus far.
- If you're assigned to lecture on a specific topic, it may be beneficial to email discussion questions to the instructor in advance, so the students can prepare for discussion.
- Bring name tags. If you'd like to generate classroom discussion, knowing the students' names is always helpful.
- If you are not assigned to a specific topic, make sure to find out what the students are reading. If you know what the students are reading, you may be able to connect your lecture to material they are already familiar with. This will make it easier for you to generate classroom discussion.
- Don't assume students are familiar with the background of your topic – take the time to explain it to them.
- Use a variety of teaching strategies and techniques to demonstrate your range. If you only lecture, it will be assumed you can do nothing else. If you say you are "learner-centered" as a teacher, ensure your teaching techniques model that commitment.

Keep in mind that you'll probably be a little disappointed with your teaching. You're used to teaching students you know in a familiar environment. So, if your teaching demonstration doesn't go as perfectly as planned, don't be too hard on yourself. Additionally, feel free to share with search committee members (who will probably ask you about your teaching) how your classes typically run and how the teaching demonstration varied from your normal routine.

Following up

After you've completed your visit, the interview isn't over just yet. We highly recommend you follow up your interview with thank-you notes. Today's job candidates commonly send thank-you notes via email to everyone on the hiring committee. While these need not be extensive notes, it is polite to send a short note that thanks committee members and the faculty for their effort, and that emphasizes your enthusiasm for the position. Sending a thank-you note assures the committee that you are genuinely interested in the position and reminds them of what a nice future colleague you would be.

Success on the job market

It is our hope that the information provided here will help readers to better anticipate and negotiate the job search process – an important rite of passage for those pursuing academic careers. It is never too early to pursue the job of your dreams!

Additional readings

Barnes, S. L. (2007) *On the Market: Strategies for a Successful Academic Job Search*, Boulder, CO: Lynne Rienner.
DeNeef, A. L., and Goodwin, C. D. (eds.) (2006) *The Academic's Handbook*, 3rd edn. Durham, NC: Duke University Press.
Vick, J. M., and Furlong, J. S. (2008) *The Academic Job Search Handbook*, 4th edn. Philadelphia, PA: University of Pennsylvania Press.

3 Money matters

The art of negotiation for women faculty

Suzanna M. Rose and Mona J. E. Danner

If "location, location, location" is the single most important consideration in real estate, the likely parallel motto for career success in academe is "Negotiate, negotiate, negotiate." Negotiation is the use of information and power to affect behavior; more specifically, it is an endeavor that focuses on gaining the favor of people from whom we want things (Cohen 1980). For women faculty, the idea of developing their negotiation skills may run counter to a well-ingrained belief that academe is a meritocracy in which rewards presumably are given to those possessing the greatest talent. In reality, few are recognized based on their expertise alone; success usually requires both job competence and the ability to negotiate. In other words, in academe as in business, "you don't get what you deserve, you get what you negotiate" (Karrass 1992).

Knowledge about how to negotiate has been shown to have a significant impact on one's likelihood of success. Those who know that negotiation requires tactical skill, as well as distinct types of information such as knowing deadlines and the other party's reputation, are generally more successful at bargaining than those who have little awareness of the task-specific components of negotiating (Stevens et al. 1993; Weingart et al. 1996). Elements of the task environment also play a role in negotiating, including the behavior of the other party, the success of attempted strategies, and the content of the task itself (Weingart et al. 1996). The other negotiator's possible gender bias has been identified as an aspect of the task environment that may significantly affect women's success as well (e.g., Gerhart and Rynes 1991). Nevertheless, actively preparing oneself for the negotiating process may help women achieve better outcomes even when the task environment is uncontrollable or unfavorable.

One of the most crucial negotiations from the standpoint of academic careers is the salary negotiation. In general, women faculty fare less well than men in this process. Research indicates that women faculty are paid lower salaries than are men – about 20 percent less, on average. Translated into dollars, colleges and universities pay women nearly $10,000 a year less than men. Gender differences remain greatest at the full professor rank, where women earn 80 percent of men's salary, but are still present at the associate and assistant professor levels, where women earn 93 percent of men's earnings. The salary gap persists across academic disciplines and types of institutions (NCES 1993, 1996; Sax et al. 1996).

Despite the importance of negotiating salary and other conditions of employment in academe, how to proceed is seldom discussed. For example, *Career Guide for Women Scholars* (Rose 1986), *The Academic Job Search Handbook* (Heiberger and Vick 1996), *Lifting a Ton of Feathers: A Woman's Guide to Surviving in the Academic World* (Caplan 1993), *Promotion and Tenure: Community and Socialization in Academe* (Tierney and Bensimon 1996), *Rhythms of Academic Life* (Frost and Taylor 1996), and *Black Women in the Academy* (Benjamin 1997) contain much information pertinent to the academic job search and how to establish and maintain a successful career, but mention little about salary or contract negotiations. The graduate school experience is similarly lacking in instruction concerning negotiation for most, although informal networks may convey relevant information from senior to junior men (e.g., Dreher and Cox 1996). As a result, new women PhDs may enter the job market with little experience or knowledge about how to position themselves for the first job. In addition, subsequent opportunities for significant salary negotiations may be infrequent in an academic career. Thus, women could be quite senior, and the wage gap with senior men quite large, before they could benefit from trial-and-error learning.

In the present chapter, our intent is to illustrate why women faculty should acquire the art of negotiating, as well as to provide practical advice concerning how to negotiate. Although faculty jobs involve numerous types of bargaining, the primary focus will be on negotiating the academic contract, with a particular emphasis on salary negotiation.

Money matters

Negotiation is important because money matters in academe. Your salary is a sign of your worth to the institution, as well as a source of self-esteem. Your economic security or that of your family also depends on your income. Moreover, your earning power affects not only your current living conditions but also your retirement benefits, which are generally calculated partly as a percentage of your base salary in the years before retirement. Thus, the most important negotiation you are likely to make during the first phase of your career is the entry-level salary negotiation. Opportunities to increase your salary throughout your career are similarly crucial for you to negotiate successfully.

The long-term financial and career implications of entry-level salary may be best illustrated with an example. Suppose a woman assistant professor, Linda, is newly hired at $42,000, and earns 93 percent (i.e., the average wage gap) of a newly hired male assistant professor, Bob, who is hired at $45,150. Now suppose both Linda and Bob get average merit raises of 5 percent for the next five years. At this juncture, when they are likely to be undergoing tenure review, the institution will have invested $17,400 more in Bob than in Linda (enough for a down payment on a house or relaxing vacations every year!). Bob also may be more enthusiastic about his job because he has been more amply rewarded and may even be seen as more valuable to the department simply because the institution has invested more in him, even though their performance has been similar. Even if the salary differential is only $1,000, the difference calculated over forty years, given 3.5 percent yearly raises, is a loss to the woman of $84,550 (Haignere 1996).

Research indicates that gender plays a role at each stage of the negotiation process that is detrimental to women. The extent and success of negotiating academic salaries depend on four steps:

- The applicant's pay expectations.
- The initial salary offered by the institution.
- Whether or not a counteroffer is made by the applicant.
- The final salary agreed upon by the applicant and the institution.

First, women tend to have lower pay expectations than do men, regardless of occupational field (Jackson et al. 1992; Major and Konar 1984). Lower salaries emerge as one consequence of lower salary expectations. For instance, applicants who conveyed lower pay expectations in one laboratory study were offered less pay than equally qualified applicants who had higher pay expectations (Major et al. 1984a). Thus, women's lower pay expectations may partly influence the second step of the negotiation, the initial salary offer.

Second, research shows that the initial salary offer given by the institution's representative (usually a White man) has a strong impact on the final outcome of negotiation (i.e., higher initial offers are associated with higher final offers). The evidence is also clear that men (particularly White men) receive better initial offers for both commercial negotiations and salary discussions than do women. In a study of car sales, Ayers (1991) found significant differences in the initial offers made by sales associates based on the buyer's gender and race. White men received lower initial price quotes than did White women and minority women and men. Experimental simulations of various retail buyer–seller interactions confirm that men procure lower prices and higher profits than do women (Neu et al. 1988). Similarly, men obtain better initial salary offers in both laboratory and field studies. Male prospects who were hypothetical job applicants were assigned higher starting salaries by research participants than were female prospects, even when they had the same qualifications and pay expectations (Major et al. 1984b). The finding of higher initial salary offers to men also held true in an investigation of the actual experiences of recent MBA graduates, who were surveyed about the outcomes of their wage discussions with employers (Gerhart and Rynes 1991).

An applicant's gender may also affect whether she or he makes one or more counteroffers during the third step of a salary negotiation and what tactics are used to negotiate. Women may have less knowledge or skill at negotiation than men. In a hypothetical salary negotiation, men college students were found to use significantly more active tactics (e.g., ask for a larger salary than that offered), whereas women were significantly more indirect in their self-promotion tactics (e.g., emphasize their motivation to work hard; Kaman and Hartel 1990). When confronted with a competitive negotiator, women MBAs in a simulated salary negotiation were less likely than men either to match this style or to use diverse negotiation tactics (Renard 1992). In one of the few studies to examine salary negotiation directly, Gerhart and Rynes (1991) found that 56 percent of the MBA students who negotiated for larger salaries received increases from $1,000 to $7,000. Although men and women showed the same proclivity to initiate salary negotiations, men received $742 more, on average, for their efforts. Propensity to negotiate also depends on the attractiveness of the offer and other options available to the applicant. If women are offered less initially, the offer may be viewed as less attractive and they may be less likely to bargain (Bacharach and Lawler 1981; Chamberlain 1955). In addition, applicants who have alternative job offers will have more bargaining power and will be more likely to negotiate (Mannix et al. 1989). Thus, a woman's skill at negotiating is not the only determinant of whether she will bargain or obtain outcomes equal to men.

The persistent wage gap between women and men in academic salaries indicates that men obtain better final salary offers at the last stage of negotiation. This difference cannot be explained solely by individual differences in ability, education, or training. Academic women's salaries lag significantly behind men's even when academic rank, type of institution, and experience are taken into account (NCES 1993). Gender stereotyping also results in the differential valuation of women and men by male supervisors with respect to vocationally relevant characteristics (Rosen and Jerdee 1978). Beliefs that women are willing to work for less pay or deserve less pay than men also remain common among administrators and supervisors (Rynes et al. 1985). Possible negotiator bias as expressed in the form of final salary offers, then, is one of the likely barriers to successful salary negotiation for women.

The first empirical study of negotiation in academe (Danner 1996) illustrates how the four steps just described operated for a national faculty sample of sociology PhDs in their first academic job. Women expected significantly lower salaries than men, initially were offered less, and were given final offers lower than those reported by men, congruent with previous research. Contrary to earlier findings, women were significantly more likely to initiate negotiations than were men. When women did not bargain, it was usually because they had been told that a higher salary simply was not possible. The major reason men did not initiate negotiations was because they were offered a salary equal to or exceeding their expectations. Despite the disparity in salary offers, it paid for both women and men to negotiate. About 92 percent of those who made a specific salary counteroffer won a salary higher than that offered initially.

In sum, the evidence concerning gender and salary negotiation indicates that women are underbenefited in terms of salary in a variety of occupations, including academe. It appears that women have little control over some aspects of the salary negotiation, such as negotiator bias with regard to the initial and final salary offer, but that high pay expectations and the use of diverse negotiating tactics translate into higher salaries for women. These results suggest that, even in adverse circumstances, women faculty may be able to improve salary negotiation outcomes by pursuing two goals: (1) developing high pay expectations and (2) planning a negotiation strategy.

Pay expectations

It is problematic enough for women faculty that administrators may give them lower initial and final salary offers than they do men, but research on gender and perceived pay entitlement indicates that women may also undervalue themselves. It has been shown that women pay themselves less than men do when asked to determine their own pay for work done in an experimental task. In one study, women and men undergraduates worked alone on a task for about an hour and were told to compensate themselves. On average, women took $2 for their work, whereas men took $3 (Major et al. 1984). Even in situations where women have outperformed a coworker, they have been found to allocate less pay to themselves (e.g., Major 1994). Research done on actual full-time workers confirms the laboratory findings, with women reporting that they deserve less pay for the jobs they held than did men (Desmarais and Curtis 1997). In addition, women have been found to work more efficiently and longer than men when paid the same amount for performing a task. For example, when women and men undergraduates were given an equal wage and told to work as long as they wished on a routine task, women accomplished more in the same time period, made fewer errors, and worked 30 percent longer than men who performed the same task (Major et al. 1984).

Part of the explanation for gender differences in pay expectations pertains to lack of information about or gender differences in available social comparison standards. At least three types of social comparisons may operate, including comparing one's current salary with male peers, female peers, or with one's own recent pay experience. First, research indicates that when women lack knowledge about male peers' earnings, they tend to have lower pay expectations (Bylsma and Major 1992). Conversely, when women receive comparison information about men's earnings, they expect to be paid equally. The first author's experience as a career consultant to women faculty at several universities suggests that many women scholars are not aware of what male peers earn. Junior women faculty typically assume that their salaries are comparable to men peers and not seek verification. Senior women faculty may not want to know peers' wages because they fear being demoralized if inequities are discovered. Not every woman knows where to look for information, either. Some are not aware that public colleges and universities make all salaries available to the public, usually through a listing obtainable at the reference desk of the campus library. Others are unfamiliar with salary scales that are regularly published by the *Chronicle of Higher Education* and the AAUP.

Comparative salary information and career support may also be lacking for women who are excluded from mentoring relationships and networks with senior men. For instance, Dreher and Cox (1996) reported that MBA graduates who had established a mentoring relationship with White men earned an average of $16,840 more than those with other mentors. However, White women and African-American and Hispanic MBAs of both genders were significantly less likely than White men to form such relationships. Thus, women may not have or seek enough information concerning male peers' salaries to allow them to negotiate effectively.

Social comparisons with female peers' salaries may be another source of women's low pay expectations. Women may be more familiar with women colleagues' salaries via informal same-sex networks. If women colleagues are also underpaid, this comparison will not reveal the top of the scale for salaries at a similar rank. Furthermore, women's pay expectations have been shown in at least one study to depend upon whether a female or male comparison group was chosen. Women in high prestige jobs were asked by Zanna et al. (1987) to indicate what they earned and to name what peers they used when making salary comparisons. Results indicated that women whose comparison group was predominantly men earned more than women whose comparison group was mixed gender or predominantly women.

One's previous pay experience has also been shown to affect pay expectations. For instance, using undergraduate students, Desmarais and Curtis (1997) demonstrated that both women and men who had higher previous income levels for their most recent job paid themselves more for completing an experimental task than did others. These results suggest that the more one earns, the more one will expect to earn. Conversely, being lower on the pay scale, as is the case for most women faculty, is likely to reduce one's initial pay expectations.

How might women faculty raise their pay expectations, then, given that low salary expectations may be internalized? We propose four strategies. First, women need to seek comparative salary information quite assiduously; in other words, you need to "do your homework." Fortunately, doing research represents an important component of our training as academics. If you are a graduate student, start preparing for the job search by learning as much as you can about the salaries of faculty at your own and comparable institutions. If you are already in a faculty position at a public institution, check regularly on peers' salaries in the library. Research indicates that the wage gap between women and men faculty is largest at private, elite institutions, where it is also most difficult to obtain information about salaries (e.g., Szafran 1984). Therefore, if you are at a private institution, you may have to rely on salary norms published annually in the *Chronicle of Higher Education* or talk about salary to peers at other universities or in similarly ranked departments at your institution. Evaluate where you stand in terms of these markers.

Second, seek multiple opinions concerning what is possible in salary negotiations as well as what is likely or usual. Do not trust any one person's opinion. The person with whom you typically negotiate (e.g., your department chair or dean) may not always be the most reliable source of information concerning what you deserve or what is possible. If he or she has offered your peers a higher entry level salary or a larger raise, he or she may justify having given you a poor bargain by impugning your performance. Because it is widely believed that academe is a meritocracy, you may also regard a below-scale salary or raise as objectively reflecting poorer quality work on your part. Verify any information concerning your salary and performance using several independent sources. Develop a network outside of your department to corroborate opinions. Women's Studies programs are often a critical source of comparative data for women faculty. It is important not to rely solely on departmental colleagues as your knowledge base because myths about what is possible sometimes get solidified within departments. For example, one of us was told by colleagues, including the department chair, that no raise was likely to accompany a promotion but was able to obtain one when negotiating directly with the dean.

Third, develop connections that will help you raise your pay expectations and improve your negotiating skill. Seek out colleagues whom you trust who have also been effective at building their careers in ways you find commendable. A colleague who is a good strategist is one who is able to answer the question "Under what conditions have exceptions to this rule, policy, or practice been made?" Conversely, a colleague who insists that "nothing can be done" to improve your salary or job conditions will not be that helpful to you. Select individuals who have high pay expectations for women, and be aware that even very high-achieving women sometimes underrate themselves or other women. For example, one of our colleagues, an extremely able woman negotiator, who had recently achieved an objective very much desired by the university, had also received another job offer at a prestigious university. She was at a point where her current dean was going to make a counteroffer. She called a friend to discuss the salary figure that would be needed to keep her, one she perceived to be extremely high. Others had told her the amount was more than she could realistically expect to get. Her friend suggested that she raise her target by at least $5,000, based on what she knew men faculty more senior to but with less responsibility than the woman were earning, even though the figure sounded high to her, as well. The woman got the money she requested as well as many other concessions, and the university got her to stay. This example demonstrates that women faculty need to learn what is "outlandish" in terms of salary, due to internalized low pay expectations, as opposed to being truly beyond market price.

In summary, women faculty with low pay expectations may need to counteract them strongly by using several strategies to raise their aspirations. By educating yourself about faculty salaries, you will develop more confidence in what you might be able to achieve.

Planning a negotiation strategy

Part of planning a specific negotiation strategy requires that you know your personal wants and professional needs, as well as how congruent these are with the mission of the institution you hope to join or are at already. This means that you should make an honest assessment of your skills, accomplishments, and potential. Every negotiator must be able to give something that is wanted by the other party. Faculty either must be able to do the job the institution perceives it needs done, or convince the other negotiator that the skills the faculty member offers are what the institution wants.

Your personal goals will help guide you in making choices about what to negotiate for and how to pursue an appropriate strategy. If you are at the job search stage, identify your personal preferences regarding the type of institution you hope to join. Teaching or research? Small or large? Geographic location? City size? Type of student body? In combination with a realistic assessment of your skills, accomplishments, and potential, the answers to these questions reveal a realistic indication of your power in negotiating during the hiring process. For example, limitations on moving due to personal or partner preference or family responsibilities will restrict one's personal job market. However, casting a narrow net and applying for positions in specific geographic regions mean that a woman will not get or be able to use another job offer to increase her bargaining power at her first-choice institution.

Assessing your situation differs to some extent for graduate students who are going on the job market versus established faculty. A tight academic job market exists in nearly every discipline. Many institutions replace retiring faculty with part-time or temporary hires, and tenure is under attack in many states. In addition to acquiring a thorough understanding of their discipline, graduate students must prepare early to position themselves as viable candidates. Job ads increasingly request some teaching experience and at least one research publication for even entry-level positions. Do your very best to get these while a student. Also, make certain that you attend professional association meetings, present your research there, meet students and faculty at other institutions, investigate the employment exchange room, and volunteer to serve on a committee. Your goal in these activities is to begin to earn recognition for yourself and develop relationships that can provide valuable information and contacts. Be aware that as a woman you may need more credentials than a man to compete effectively for the same job.

Planning for tenured senior faculty also necessitates an assessment of how one's talents fit the institution's mission, how one is progressing toward promotion to full professor or toward other professional goals, and one's likely marketability. Because senior faculty cost more to hire, few jobs are advertised at the senior level, and the competition for them is quite stiff. The average tenured faculty may not have much chance of getting a job elsewhere, and this will limit her bargaining power with administrators. A woman's personal life (e.g., spouse employed, children in school) more so than a man's may be seen by administrators as reducing the likelihood that she would seriously consider leaving. Senior women who seek to negotiate a better contract at their current institution must confront the assumption that they will not really leave if their requests are not met. If you are tenured and not marketable or not planning on moving, one of the most effective ways to increase your salary is to assume administrative responsibilities (e.g., Lewis 1975). On the other hand, if you are a highly successful scholar who wishes to promote her research career, seriously applying for jobs may help you to find a better one or use a job offer at another institution to improve your current situation.

Knowing what to negotiate for is equally important. We emphasize base salary because salary is forever. However, there are numerous things you may need – not want, but need – to do the job the institution wants you to do. These will be discussed more fully in the next section on the negotiation process.

Thus, planning a negotiation strategy begins first with knowing what you want and need and knowing the institution with which you're dealing. Both require thoughtful consideration and extensive research before any initial offer is received or sought. Once you have identified your goals as described above, you are ready to move on to planning the actual negotiation strategy.

Planning the negotiation strategy itself requires that you carefully analyze the total situation and the goals on which you have decided in light of three tightly interrelated variables: power, information, and time (Cohen 1980). It is also important to realize that a negotiation is a process, not a single event, that involves all three in concert.

Power

Power is defined as the capacity or ability to get things done; to influence others to think or do what you would like them to do; or to exercise control over people, events, situations, or oneself. The concept of power sometimes has a negative connotation to women, particularly the notion of having coercive power over someone. However, power also has many positive aspects that are important to keep in mind (e.g., power is required to implement one's goals and facilitate one's own and others' development). Several types of power that are relevant to negotiating will be discussed below, including self-confidence and persistence; expert power; and the power of investment, identification, and formal procedures.

Self-confidence, or the perception of one's own power, will enhance your power in any negotiation. Granted, it is not easy to perceive yourself as personally powerful if you have been discriminated against, disregarded, or otherwise treated badly. The cumulative effect of a hostile environment cannot be ignored as a factor that affects the self-esteem and career confidence of women graduate students and faculty. If you feel demoralized or inadequate in your role as a professional, you may need to obtain a considerable amount of support in order to present yourself in a positive and self-confident manner. Women have reported finding this kind of support through role playing, creative visualization, feminist support networks and professional organizations, and therapy. Presenting yourself in a positive way requires that you honestly appraise how you come across to others through a process of self-examination, seeking feedback from supportive others, and getting the help you need to build self-confidence.

A self-defeating self-presentation that has been observed among some women job candidates by one of the authors is when the candidate's first move is to enumerate her weakness for the current position. The strategy was used by a candidate who had numerous recent publications and a considerable amount of federal funding for her work. Early in her interview with various individual faculty, the candidate stated that she knew she hadn't published as much as she should have in the past few years. By framing her performance in a negative light, the candidate provided a "lens" for the review of her work that was to her detriment. It is a much better idea to focus on your strengths in any negotiation and leave the responsibility for finding your supposed weaknesses to the other side.

It is also wise in terms of projecting self-confidence to review your probable limitations for the position for which you are applying and consider ways they may be either deemphasized or turned into a source of power and strength. Do not leave it solely to your interviewers or colleagues to determine your contribution. You are a major player in influencing how your work is viewed. For instance, perhaps your publication record is not up to competitive standards in terms of quantity. It is important, then, to provide information about the high quality of your work, such as including rejection rates of journals in which you publish, the ranking of journals or presses in which your work appears, or citation counts or favorable reviews of your publications. Or perhaps you have published less because you do time-consuming field research instead of laboratory studies. You may want to point out that recent trends in your area indicate that field research is the "cutting edge." Always be prepared to educate your colleagues about your contribution. Few faculty have time to read much outside their own area, so it is important not to assume they know a lot more about what you're doing than what you tell them.

An aspect of power that is related to self-confidence is persistence. According to Cohen (1980: 83), "Most people aren't persistent enough when negotiating." This may apply especially to women. For instance, some of the women faculty in Danner's (1996) research did not bargain because they were told that the offer they had been given was nonnegotiable. However, other research has shown that individuals who bargained for salary increases in response to a nonnegotiable offer generally obtained a higher final offer (Gerhart and Rynes 1991). Persistence also refers to holding one's position over time. Be prepared to make a case on your own behalf more than once, perhaps even over a period of years. The "squeaky wheel" strategy works. Most people who may find it easy to say No once or even several times may find it difficult to do so continually and may eventually grant some concessions.

A second type of power that is highly valued in academe is expert power. Presumably, an outstanding or solid scholarly reputation will be justly rewarded by your institution. Expert power is likely to provide one of your strongest power bases; however, it does not automatically translate into better job conditions for women faculty, who often work harder and longer than men to get the salary and recognition they deserve for comparable work. For instance, Wenneras and Wold (1997) found that reviewers for postdoctoral fellowships in biomedicine in Sweden had consistently given female applicants lower scores than equally productive men. The researchers reported that, in some cases, the women applicants would have had to publish three extra papers in top-tier journals or twenty extra papers in less prestigious journals to be ranked the same as the male applicants. Likewise, research on admissions to the National Academy of Sciences indicated that, on average, women were admitted nine years later than men, even though the research that led to their election did not appear to be done any later (Zuckerman and Cole 1975).

With these caveats in mind, expert power as reflected by your competitive standing in the job market still provides one of the major bargaining points in an academic salary negotiation. Having other institutions interested in hiring you provides verification of your credentials. Although you are in the strongest position to negotiate when you have another job offer in hand, some faculty have used the job application process effectively to negotiate at earlier stages. For example, one woman, Jane, had received a job offer at one university and was deliberating over whether to accept it. In the meantime, she had been called for an interview by another institution. She used the second institution's interest in her to raise her counteroffer to the first school, and successfully negotiated a higher salary and better terms of employment than had been offered.

The investment that the institution and specific individuals have made in you is another source of power. In any hiring situation, the department and university will have spent a considerable amount of time and money to consider you for a position before offering you the job. After such an investment, most of the people running the job search may prefer not to start over with a new candidate and will probably try quite hard to meet reasonable requests (e.g., extend the deadline for considering the contract, provide additional resources). If you are a senior faculty member, administrators will be looking for evidence that they have gotten a good return on their investment from you before being willing to invest more. Develop ways to educate relevant administrators about what you have accomplished. For example, you might send a note to your department chair, dean, or chair of the funding committee about an article or book you wrote or got published during a leave or summer fellowship funded by your institution. Keeping a few key people informed of your successes will also make it easier to approach them later if you need allies when seeking a promotion, raise, grant, sabbatical, or whatever. The more familiar they are with your work, the more effectively they will be able to advocate for you.

Others' identification with you is yet another source of power that influences the negotiation process. This power base may be less available for women faculty to use than men with regard to superiors, who also are likely to be male. Research indicates that women are often excluded from informal networks and protégé relationships in the professions (e.g., Clark and Corcoran 1986; Dreher and Cox 1996; Zuckerman et al. 1991). Dreher and Cox (1996) have pointed out that individual characteristics such as race and gender are of considerable importance in understanding how existing opportunity structures work. Sexual orientation and class background might be added to this list, as well. Opportunity structures are influenced by these characteristics because influential decision makers (who are mostly White men) are more likely to form close relationships with individuals who are similar to themselves (other White men; Dreher and Cox 1996). Thus, White men will have more access to and benefit more from relationships with powerful White men in academe than will White women, women or men of color, lesbians, women faculty from poor or working-class economic backgrounds, or someone with a combination of these identities (e.g., Gregory 1995; Tokarczyk and Fay 1993).

The way the power of identification with similar others may work to the detriment of women faculty may be illustrated with two actual case examples. The first case pertained to two women faculty hired by the same department in the same year, one White and one African-American. The older White men in the department identified more strongly with the White woman than with the African-American woman, who intimidated them by her outspokenness. The White woman was labeled the "star" of the two, even though both had graduated from prestigious institutions and had similar records. The department chair gave the White women her preferred courses to teach, which were in her research area and involved little course preparation. Against department policy, the African-American woman was given an above-average course load and numerous new courses to prepare, none of which was in her research area. This problem was not corrected until higher administration became aware of it. Besides demonstrating race discrimination, this example shows that the identification of the White woman as "like us" worked in her favor, whereas the social distance between the African-American woman and the White male faculty made it easier for them to disregard her concerns. In a second case, a department chair (a White man) went to the dean (also a White man) to advocate successfully for a higher salary for a younger White male faculty member with whom he played golf. The younger man said he needed a raise because his wife had just had a baby. The department chair refused to advocate for a raise for the young man's similarly accomplished female colleague, who was the sole supporter of her husband and child at the time. In order to get a raise, she had to go on to the job market, obtain an invitation to interview, and bargain with the dean herself. It is reasonable to conclude that the older man's identification with the younger man's role as a provider played a part in his advocacy for the man, but was not a motivator in the woman's case.

Given that women faculty may have difficulty becoming "one of the boys," they may have to rely on power bases other than identification. Those who are ineligible for recruitment into the elite based on gender, race, sexual orientation, or class are in a position similar to that of a dissenting male scholar who has been judged not to fit in. According to Lewis (1975), such individuals will be left to make their own career; it is only in this case that the rule of publish or perish will be operative. Otherwise, there is little evidence that one's publication record is tied to faculty rank or salaries (e.g., Doering 1972; Lewis 1975; Szafran 1984). The four possible outcomes for the dissenting scholar, then, are:

> First, he [*sic*] may voluntarily leave the department. Second, if he fails to engage in any scholarly activity, he may be asked to leave, regardless of his skill in the classroom. Third, he may become an industrious scholar, put a minimum amount of effort into his teaching and other departmental responsibilities, and be harassed, or treated unfairly; eventually he may leave to maintain his self-respect. Fourth, he may become a productive scholar and a skilled teacher, and since his senior colleagues would be flagrantly violating academic norms by denying promotion or tenure, he can expect eventually to receive either or both.
>
> (Lewis 1975: 41)

Although it has been more than twenty years since Lewis described these outcomes, they describe the options for many women faculty today very well. They also suggest that, because they lack identification power with the gatekeepers, women would do well to enhance their expert power as much as possible to achieve the fourth outcome.

Formal procedures constitute a last power base for women that will be discussed here. At times, women faculty have been forced to use grievances and legal remedies to maintain their rights. Because of the emotional and financial cost of such actions, it is preferable to negotiate using other strategies, if possible. It is also best to forgo using the threat of initiating a formal procedure when bargaining; to do so is likely to shut down the negotiation. However, to indicate that you are concerned about the "equity" or "fairness" of salary or contract decisions suggests that you see your rights as being violated and implies that you may pursue the matter further if not satisfied. Providing clear evidence of your performance in comparison with that of better-paid male (or White) colleagues could demonstrate that you have a strong case for a grievance or other action. Most savvy administrators will realize that it would be better to take care of your situation at this point rather than later. Grievance panels in faculty–administration disputes at most universities tend toward compromise, so if you go to the effort to conduct a grievance, there is a good chance you will get something you request. Due to the high personal cost of this strategy and possible (illegal) retaliation, it is recommended only as a last resort. It is also wise, when pursuing this option, to seek legal advice.

Time

Most people tend to think of the time frame of a negotiation as that period in which the actual bargaining takes place. In fact, the negotiation often involves a much longer process. If you are looking for a job, you may already have laid a series of connections by using your network to locate openings or influence perceptions of your application. Once you are hired, you will have an ongoing relationship with many people with whom you will negotiate. This means that you and the other party may have considerable information about each other and a history with which you will have to contend. Your strategy should take this longer timeline into account. You also will need to know or should learn the formal and informal deadlines for making requests, so as to time your actions appropriately. Asking for a raise after all the funds have been distributed is not likely to yield the outcome you desire and will make you appear naive. Keep in mind that you may need to develop a strategy that involves repeated contacts over several years to get your desired goals. Finally, recognize that time may require you to change your strategy, because circumstances change with time. Keep an open mind and be flexible.

Information

The information you gather before the formal negotiation itself will be crucial to the outcome you achieve. Most of the information you will need will have to be obtained by word of mouth from your network. Thus, the benefits of developing a university-wide and national network cannot be overestimated. Several types of information you will need to be a successful negotiator have already been described in the earlier discussion on pay expectations, including learning peers' salaries at your own and comparable institutions, what exceptions there have been, and under what circumstances they were granted. Two types of information that have been useful to the authors in addition to those described earlier include information about precedence and about the other party's or institution's needs. First, finding there has been a precedent for a specific action has helped a number of women known to one author to obtain maternity leaves or have the tenure clock stopped. In one instance, a woman was told by her department chair that, because there was no official maternity leave policy, she would have to teach that semester. When the woman learned that someone else in another department had been granted an unofficial maternity leave by the chair, she went to the dean to negotiate a similar leave for herself. In another case, a woman who had two children in the years before the tenure decision (and no maternity leave) was given a negative tenure vote by her department. When she established that a precedent had been set for other women in some departments to stop the tenure clock during a maternity leave, she was able retroactively to receive a two-year stop in the tenure clock. Two years later, she obtained tenure.

Second, having information about the other party's needs may be invaluable in a negotiation. For example, one woman colleague who was negotiating with a chancellor to retain funding for an endowed professorship had heard immediately prior to the meeting that the chancellor had endorsed a new research initiative for the university aimed at getting more federal funding. The woman was able to argue successfully with the chancellor to keep the endowed professorship funding at a high level based on the argument that cuts would make it difficult to attract faculty who had federal funding for the position, subsequently jeopardizing the chancellor's goals.

In summary, planning the negotiation requires that you identify your personal and professional goals and incorporate them into a strategy that uses your strongest power bases and the information you have gathered over a period of time to achieve your goals. In the next section, the tactics that can be used to implement your strategy will be explained.

The negotiation process

The process of coming to agreement about salary and other terms of the academic contract is often correctly described as a game. Some tactics that may be used in playing the negotiating game will be described below using: (1) case studies, (2) examples of items that have been negotiated successfully by women faculty, and (3) a step-by-step description of the negotiation process.

Case studies

The two case studies in Box 3.1 provide a more in-depth picture of how the actual bargaining session is conducted. The two cases chosen show how the process occurred for actual women faculty, one at the hiring stage of her career, and one negotiating for a raise at the senior level. In case study 1, Susan was able to achieve a successful negotiation by using several strategies. First, because the offer was given late in the season, the timing of the negotiation was in her favor. Other candidates for the position might have taken other offers, making her bargaining position more favorable. Second, the institution had already shown its willingness to make an investment in her, so it was only a small step for the dean to take to make increases in the investment in order to secure a top-ranked candidate. Third, the example illustrates that the dean was prepared to negotiate even though he described the offer as nonnegotiable. Lastly, Susan's enthusiasm conveyed that she was likely to accept the position if her offer was met.

Box 3.1 The bargaining process: two case studies

Case study 1

Susan was offered a tenure-track assistant professor position following her interview at a nationally recognized PhD program. The dean told Susan that the $35,000 salary was at the high end of the range and that it, and the $500 moving expenses allowance, were nonnegotiable. She was given ten days to think about it. Although she wanted the job very much and thought that the offer was a fair one, Susan's mentor encouraged her to make a counteroffer. He explained to her that it would cost her nothing, that the hiring institution had very few women faculty in the program, and that it was already mid-March. He also reminded her that she was a good candidate with some teaching and research experience. (During graduate school, Susan had worked on her mentor's grant, which had produced two minor coauthored publications, and had taught two introductory courses. Although "all but dissertation," or "ABD," she would finish the dissertation before starting the faculty job.)

Susan took her mentor's advice and, after ten days, asked for a salary of $37,000 and moving expenses of $1,500. Also, for the first time, she requested specific computer hardware and software, graduate faculty status, and guaranteed summer teaching. In making the requests, Susan followed her mentor's advice and emphasized her experience, her research agenda, and her excitement at coming to the program and working with graduate students. The dean countered with a salary of $36,500 and moving expenses of $1,000, all the computer equipment requested, and graduate faculty status. He said Susan would probably be able to teach in the summer but was unable to guarantee it. The dean was cordial throughout the negotiations and never reminded Susan that he had earlier said that his offer was not negotiable. Susan accepted the offer.

Case study 2

Ruth had been at her institution for about fifteen years and had just been promoted to full professor. As is typical in the case of many senior faculty, salary inversion had resulted in her salary being close to the level of that of many newly hired faculty. This occurs when merit raises for established faculty fail to keep pace with the salaries for new hires, which must be at market level in order to be competitive. Ruth's reputation as a feminist activist had also done little to endear her to the department chair. Thus, even though Ruth's publication record was similar to male peers', her salary had fallen well below theirs. Ruth planned to request a "salary adjustment" from the dean once she obtained final confirmation of her promotion. If she did not receive her requested increase, she planned to file a grievance.

Ruth first approached her chair with a list of faculty salaries (obtained from the library) for faculty at similar rank in the social sciences to demonstrate that a considerable increase would be required to bring her salary into line. Ruth named $58,000 as her target figure for the following year, an amount $2,000 over what her most immediate male peer would earn. The chair sent her to the dean to negotiate, but did not offer to accompany her. The dean said he would not discuss salary until the following month. Ruth made her points concerning her performance and the issue of equity anyway. She also gave the salary data to the director of another program on campus of which she was a faculty member, and asked that person to advocate for her as well. In the meantime, the chair told Ruth that she would "never get" the figure she had requested.

A month later, Ruth again met with the dean. She reviewed her performance, using her recent promotion to indicate that her work was nationally recognized. She also let the dean know that she was aware that a faculty grievance by a colleague who was less productive than herself had been settled in the colleague's favor. The dean offered to increase her salary over a three-year period. Ruth had calculated an amount three years hence that would place her $2,000 ahead of her most immediate peer and named that as her target figure. Several offers and counteroffers were made, and Ruth accepted as the final offer a salary that would place her $1,000 above her target goal.

The situation for Ruth as a senior faculty in case study 2 was quite different. Ruth had a considerable amount of information about how the dean had operated in the past and what other faculty earned. She planned her raise strategy to correspond with a promotion and linked her request to a pay equity issue rather than using a strictly merit raise approach. Knowing that she had little support from the department chair, Ruth found another ally for her cause in the director of another program on campus of which she was a faculty member. Ruth also refused to let the chair's pessimism about an increase affect her target salary figure. The fact that the dean met twice with Ruth and once with both the chair and director about Ruth's salary may have worked in her favor by increasing the time investment the dean had made in her. Ruth was also able to convey the seriousness of her intent by mentioning her peer's salary grievance, thereby implying she might consider other avenues if her request was not met. However, throughout the negotiation, Ruth maintained an upbeat, professional attitude about herself and the university that seemed to be appreciated by the dean.

The two case studies demonstrate that each negotiation is unique and may involve quite different goals and tactics. No one formula may be applied to every negotiation.

Negotiable items in an academic contract

Once you have identified your personal and professional goals, you must translate these into specific requests in the negotiation. Although base salary is the most important negotiation, there are many hidden expenses involved in living the academic life that may become part of the negotiation process. Other forms of financial compensation and personal satisfaction may come in the form of other benefits you may be able to negotiate. Ask yourself what you need from the institution in order to fulfill your professional goals, and then consider what you need to fulfill the institution's goals for you. Laboratory space? Few service requirements? Computer equipment? We have compiled a list of things below that you may be able to negotiate for in addition to base salary. The negotiation for these items should occur after you have been offered the job. Everything you request above the initial offer made to you should be justified in terms of getting the job done that the institution wants you to do. All of the items listed below were obtained by assistant professors in actual negotiations, though not all for the same job.

- Base salary increases (most important).
- Moving expenses.
- Higher rank.
- Office specifications (e.g., window, central location, size).
- Startup money for research (e.g., cost of laboratory or equipment).
- Research space.
- Graduate or undergraduate student assistants.
- Summer supplements for teaching or research.
- Computer equipment, including software and printer.
- Conference and/or research travel expenses.
- Reduced teaching load, at least during first or second year.
- Agreement to repeat courses annually to reduce number of new course preparations.
- Two-day-per-week teaching schedule.
- Reduced service expectations (but be cautious).
- Spousal or partner hire.
- Time toward tenure reduced.

If it is your first job, realistically appraise the contradictions inherent in the items above, especially those surrounding teaching and service. Although your institution may privilege solitary research, remember that first impressions matter. For example, new faculty who are frequently in the office are seen by faculty and students and able to develop relationships and reputations. Likewise, service on committees demonstrates one's competence and citizenship.

At the senior level, negotiations can be quite complex. If you are being considered for another job or have been offered another job, and your current institution is eager to keep you, you may be able to bargain for a number of additional benefits that may be limited only by your creativity. Some actual benefits that have been obtained by various senior faculty in this situation are listed below:

- A considerable salary increase.
- Promotion from associate to full professor.
- Ample funding for startup of research program or laboratory.
- Funds to build a program(s), including other faculty positions.
- Postdoctoral fellow positions for research program.
- Funding or fellowships for graduate students.
- Funding for colloquium series.

- Space for self and research staff.
- Resources for journal editorship role.
- New building or reconfiguration of current space.
- Journal subscriptions or other library resources.

Once you have decided on what possible items you might want, prioritize your list into two or three categories, including what items are essential to you, which are moderately important, and which are your "dream list." Now you are prepared to negotiate using the steps below.

Steps in the negotiation process

After you have done the preparation described in this chapter, you should be ready to proceed with implementing your strategy in the actual bargaining session. Below, we suggest some general rules and steps in the negotiation process, and we provide a cautionary note to accompany them. Every situation is different. You may break nearly every rule and still be very successful, though that would be the exceptional case. Perhaps the most important rules are to be reasonably flexible and most gracious. Flexibility demonstrates your interest in serving the institution as well as yourself. A professional attitude assures that good feelings about you will persist despite the outcome. Academe is a very small community and one in which you need to maintain an excellent reputation. Unfortunately, many women (and men) encounter negotiators who are neither flexible nor gracious. In those cases, if you are in the hiring process, we suggest viewing this as an important insight into the nature of the administrator and institution and the likely conditions of work.

- *Set goals.* Set a high explicit goal for the negotiation based on your homework. Be sure this goal is high enough; do not underestimate yourself. The goal should be higher than the minimum you are prepared to accept.
- *Conduct the negotiation in person,* if possible. In the hiring process, telephone negotiations are common, but it is generally recommended that negotiations be conducted in person even if they involve more expense (Cohen 1980). Face-to-face interactions are less likely to result in misunderstandings, are more informal, more collaborative, longer, and make it harder to say No. If the negotiation must take place over the telephone, you are in the best position if you plan the call carefully beforehand and are the caller, not the one called.
- *Let the other party name the first figure.* The first dollar amount mentioned sets either the floor or the ceiling for future negotiations. In hiring situations, the institution sets a salary range for a particular position, and it behooves the candidate to find out what the range is early on. This should be done as discreetly as possible. Some shrewd negotiators may attempt to pressure the candidate to name "what it will take to get you here" during the interview process before even offering her the job, especially if they

perceive the candidate to be uncomfortable with negotiating. Immediate agreement with your named salary is likely to indicate that the administrator was playing a game and has won. We have heard many stories like this. Indeed, one of the authors had this experience. She politely refused to name a figure by asking about the salary range and stated that she had not yet learned the local cost of living, tax structure, or other benefits. The administrator persisted in asking her. After four rounds of this, and clearly exasperated, he named the figure that was her actual expected salary. She feigned disappointment and stated that it was below her expectations.

Resist the pressure to name a figure first, particularly in a hiring situation where you may have little knowledge about the salary structure. Instead, wait to begin negotiations until you are offered a specific job at a stated salary. Then counter the offer with a higher one, a full justification for why you are worth the extra money, and other items you need in order to do your job. The only exception to this rule generally occurs among more senior job candidates or current faculty who know exactly what it will take to get or keep them, know that the institution has paid comparable wages to peers, can justify their worth, and are prepared to stand firm.

- *Remember that almost everything is negotiable.* Nonnegotiable final offers, deadlines, and a host of other rules that have been legitimized by being put in writing or strongly asserted may nevertheless be negotiated under the "right" circumstances (Cohen 1980; Nierenberg 1981). For instance, one of the authors received a grant from her institution that specified in bold type that if the same proposal was funded elsewhere the funds must be returned to the institution. When she received funding from another source, she casually mentioned to a colleague that she was going to return the first grant award. She then learned that it was possible to negotiate to keep funds from the first grant if she had a "good reason," despite the rule, and was successful in keeping part of the funding.
- *Be self-confident.* Convey the message that you will not back down on your negotiation position. Be confident that you are worth what you are requesting. Flexibility should only come into play when the negotiation seems to require it in order to keep it moving. At this point, be certain that the institution offers the same degree of flexibility as it requests of you.
- *Use persuasive arguments.* Use substantive arguments to persuade the other person to change her or his mind about an issue. For instance, perhaps you have not been the top-ranked faculty member in your department in terms of publications over the past few years, but you have consistently been publishing above the department mean for a number of years. You might argue that a greater than average raise is warranted in your case as recognition for "sustained superior contribution." Emphasize all the skills you bring to the institution.
- *Exchange information.* Get information about the other person's preferences on a specific issue, either by asking directly what issue is most important ("What consideration have you given to my two years' postdoctoral

experience in your salary offer?" "To what extent have you taken my record of federal funding into account?") or by indirectly judging the other's reactions to your offers.

- *Approach the negotiation as a win–win event.* Assume that your gain will be beneficial to the other person, and, if possible, make this reasoning part of the negotiation process. For example, you might argue that it is advantageous for the university hiring you to pay you at the upper end of the assistant professor scale because you are already a seasoned teacher and researcher who will be able to pull her weight in the department immediately.
- *Tradeoff issues.* Be prepared to trade off issues that are lower in value to you for issues that have higher value. For instance, it may be wise to negotiate for a reduced teaching load rather than a guaranteed summer teaching appointment to increase your income, in order to provide more time for research in your schedule. Likewise, a higher salary is preferable to a better computer when the extant one will do.
- *Attention to time.* Two aspects of time are important. First, a new faculty's starting salary may well affect her for the rest of her career, especially once she is "tenured in" or otherwise place-bound. Indeed, this may be the most opportune time of one's career to negotiate salary, because new salaries frequently come from the university's budget line, whereas adjustments for current faculty often come from within departmental resources. In addition, the hiring institution may be willing to offer a good beginning salary in order to compete successfully with other universities. Moreover, recent graduates enter their first jobs with many positives; their graduate school success lies behind them and their potential before them. Current faculty have established and often complex reputations within their institutions and disciplines. Few people negotiate the terrain of academe, indeed of life itself, without ruffling a few feathers, including some that belong to influential administrators or scholars. Thus, current faculty may need to initiate salary negotiation in concert with some significant milestone, such as a promotion, a recent grant award or other type of scholarly recognition, and possibly even news of a salary grievance that has been settled in favor of someone in a position similar to yours.

  Second, knowing the employer's timetable in a hiring situation and gracefully stretching it to its limits increases the institution's investment in a job candidate. Generally, faculty and administrators make job offers only to people they want and need, a decision they have come to following a lengthy and painstaking process that may not be completed until near the end of the academic year. Thus, ask for time to make your decisions regarding a job offer, and remember that even time can be negotiated.

In summary, successful negotiation requires that you utilize power, time, and information effectively within the context of the actual negotiating session, as described above.

Conclusion

It is important to realize that the effectiveness of your negotiation skill cannot be judged solely by the dollar outcome or additional benefits of the bargain you obtain. Women faculty experience serious salary inequities in academe, regardless of their performance. Research consistently indicates that discrimination is more severe at the later stages of women professors' careers than at the recruitment stage (i.e., recruitment equity is easier to obtain than rank or salary equity for women; Szafran 1984). These findings suggest that women faculty have their best chance to achieve equity during the hiring process and should carefully plan their negotiation strategy before the job search. They also indicate that senior women will be required to do some hard negotiating at later stages of their careers if they hope to reduce the gender salary gap by a significant amount. In other words, negotiation may not necessarily result in a "win" with you earning more than others; it may just keep you from falling as far behind as you might.

The positive aspects of negotiation for women extend far beyond the actual outcome of the deal, and it is these we wish to emphasize in this chapter. By accepting responsibility for what you can do to advance yourself, you are likely to feel more self-confident and satisfied with your job, as well as to obtain better outcomes for yourself. In addition, self-blame is likely to be reduced by the realization that your negotiating skill alone may not be sufficient to counteract sex discrimination. Finally, as women faculty become more aware that, as a group, they are disadvantaged in the salary process, we hope there will be a collaborative response to improve the situation for women as a whole on their campuses. One strategy is for women faculty to conduct their own faculty salary study. Lois Haignere (1996) successfully implemented such a strategy with twenty-nine New York State universities using a procedure described in *Pay Checks: A Guide to Achieving Salary Equity in Higher Education*. The result was a $2 million settlement for women and minority faculty. Similar individual and collective efforts to challenge pay inequity should eventually strengthen women's position at the negotiating table.

Note

Reprinted with permission from *Arming Athena: Career Strategies for Women Academics*, edited by Lynn Collins, Kathryn Quina, and Joan Chrisler (Thousand Oaks, CA: Sage, 1998).

References

Ayers, I. (1991) "Fair driving: Gender and race discrimination in retail car negotiations," *Harvard Law Review*, 104: 817–72.

Bacharach, S. B., and Lawler, E. J. (1981) *Bargaining*. San Francisco, CA: Jossey-Bass.

Benjamin, L. (ed.) (1997) *Black Women in the Academy: Promises and Perils*. Gainesville, FL: University of Florida Press.

Bylsma, W. H., and Major, B. (1992) "Two routes to eliminating gender differences in personal entitlement," *Psychology of Women Quarterly*, 16: 193–200.

Caplan, P. (1993) *Lifting a Ton of Feathers: A Woman's Guide to Surviving in the Academic World*. Toronto, Ont.: University of Toronto Press.

Chamberlain, N. W. (1955) *A General Theory of Economic Progress*. New York: Harper.

Clark, S. M., and Corcoran, M. (1986) "Perspectives on the professional socialization of women faculty: A case of accumulative disadvantage?" *Journal of Higher Education*, 57: 20–43.

Cohen, H. (1980) *You Can Negotiate Anything*. New York: Bantam Books.

Danner, Mona J. E. (1996) Gender and the Process of Negotiating the Academic Contract. Unpublished research.

Desmarais, S., and Curtis, J. (1997) "Gender and perceived pay entitlement: Testing for effects of experience with income," *Journal of Personality and Social Psychology*, 72: 141–50.

Doering, R. (1972) "Publish or perish: Book productivity and academic rank at twenty-six elite universities," *American Sociologist*, 7: 11–13.

Dreher, G. F., and Cox, T. H., Jr. (1996) "Race, gender, and opportunity: A study of compensation attainment and the establishment of mentoring relationships," *Journal of Applied Psychology*, 81: 287–308.

Frost, P. J., and Taylor, M. S. (1996) *Rhythms of Academic Life*. Thousand Oaks, CA: Sage.

Gerhart, B., and Rynes, S. (1991) "Determinants and consequences of salary negotiations by graduating male and female MBAs," *Journal of Applied Psychology*, 76: 256–62.

Gregory, S. T. (1995) *Black Women in the Academy: The Secrets to Success*. Lanham, MD: University Press of America.

Haignere, L. (1996) *Pay Checks: A Guide to Achieving Salary Equity in Higher Education*. Albany, NY: United University Professions, Local 2190.

Heiberger, M. and Vick, J. M. (1996) *The Academic Job Search Handbook*, 2nd edn. Philadelphia, PA: University of Pennsylvania.

Jackson, L. A., Gardner, P. D., and Sullivan, L. A. (1992) "Explaining gender differences in self-pay expectations: Social comparison standards and perceptions of fair pay," *Journal of Applied Psychology*, 77: 651–63.

Kaman, B. D., and Hartel, C. E. J. (1990) "Anticipating pay negotiation strategies and pay outcomes during recruitment: An exploration of gender differences." Paper presented at the annual meeting of the Academy of Management, San Francisco, August.

Karrass, C. L. (1992) *The Negotiating Game*. New York: Harper.

Lewis, L. (1975) *Scaling the Ivory Tower*. Baltimore, MD: Johns Hopkins University Press.

Major, B. (1994) "From disadvantage to deserving: Comparisons, justifications and the psychology of entitlement," in M. P. Zanna (ed.) *Advances in Experimental Social Psychology*, Vol. 26. New York: Academic Press, 293–355.

Major, B., and Konar, E. (1984) "An investigation of sex differences in pay expectations and their possible causes," *Academy of Management Journal*, 27: 777–92.

Major, B., McFarlin, D., and Gagnon, D. (1984a) "Overworked and underpaid: On the nature of gender differences in personal entitlement," *Journal of Personality and Social Psychology*, 47: 1399–412.

Major, B., Vanderslice, B., and McFarlin, D. B. (1984b) "Effects of pay expected on pay received: The confirmatory nature of initial expectations," *Journal of Applied Social Psychology*, 14: 399–412.

Mannix, E. A., Thompson, L. L., and Bazerman, M. H. (1989) "Negotiation in small groups," *Journal of Applied Psychology*, 74: 508–17.

NCES (1993) *Salaries of Full-time Instructional Faculty on Nine- and Ten-month Contracts in Institutions of Higher Education, 1982–1983 through 1992–1993*. Washington, DC: U.S. Department of Education.

NCES (National Center for Education Statistics) (1996) *Salaries of Full-time Instructional Faculty, 1994–1995*. Washington, DC: U.S. Department of Education.

Neu, J., Graham, J., and Gilly, M. (1988) "The influence of gender on behaviors and outcomes in a retail buyer–seller negotiation simulation," *Journal of Retailing*, 64: 427–51.

Nierenberg, G. I. (1981) *The Art of Negotiating*. New York: Pocket Books.

Renard, M. K. (1992) Salary Negotiations and the Male–Female Wage Gap. Unpublished doctoral dissertation, University of Maryland.

Rose, S. (ed.) (1986) *Career Guide for Women Scholars*. New York: Springer.

Rosen, B., and Jerdee, T. H. (1978) "Perceived sex differences in managerially relevant characteristics," *Sex Roles*, 4: 837–43.

Rynes, S. L., Rosen, B., and Mahoney, T. A. (1985) "Evaluating comparable worth: Three perspectives," *Business Horizons*, 28: 82–86.

Sax, L., Astin, A. W., Arrendondo, M., and Korn, W. S. (1996) *The American College Teacher: National Norms for the 1996–1996 HERI Faculty Survey*. Los Angeles, CA: Higher Education Research Institute.

Stevens, C. K., Bavetta, A. G., and Gist, M. E. (1993) "Gender differences in the acquisition of salary negotiation skills: The role of goals, self-efficacy, and perceived control," *Journal of Applied Psychology*, 78: 723–35.

Szafran, R. F. (1984) *Universities and Women Faculty: Why some Organizations Discriminate more than Others*. New York: Praeger.

Tierney, W. G., and Bensimon, E. M. (1996) *Promotion and Tenure: Community and Socialization in Academe*. Albany, NY: State University of New York Press.

Tokarczyk, M. M., and Fay, E. A. (eds) (1993) *Working Class Women in the Academy: Laborers in the Knowledge Factory*. Amherst, MA: University of Massachusetts Press.

Weingart, L., Hyder, E. B., and Prietula, M. J. (1996) "Knowledge matters: The effect of tactical descriptions on negotiation behavior and outcome," *Journal of Personality and Social Psychology*, 70: 1205–17.

Wenneras, C., and Wold, A. (1997) "Nepotism and sexism in peer-review," *Nature*, 387 (6631), 341–43, May 22.

Zanna, M. P., Crosby, F., and Lowenstein, G. (1987) "Male reference groups and discontent among female professionals," in B. Gutek and L. Larwood (eds) *Women's Career Development*. Beverly Hills, CA: Sage, 28–41.

Zuckerman, H., and Cole, J. R. (1975) "Women in American science," *Minerva*, 13: 82–102.

Zuckerman, H., Cole, J. R., and Bruer, J. T. (eds) (1991) *The Outer Circle: Women in the Scientific Community*. New York: Norton.

4 Being a new faculty

Angela M. Moe and Lisa M. Murphy

For many an academic, the transition between graduate school and a faculty appointment, while exciting, is also a period fraught with anxiety, self-doubt, and isolation. Having identified themselves as graduate students for several years, and thus enjoying the relative comfort and predictability that may be found in such a status, it is often quite daunting to launch into the unknown role of faculty member. This is not to suggest graduate school is easy; it is anything but easy, as outlined in Chapter 1. However, it is often the case that graduate school provides a bit more structure in terms of one's working environment, within which students usually have a decent sense of what is expected of them and when. A sense of community may also be easier to come by within graduate school, as scholars find themselves surrounded by others who are going through many of the same courses, exams, and related processes. Alternatively, completing one's degree and moving on to an assistant professor type of position brings with it many uncertainties and questions, with seemingly few outlets to rely upon for guidance, support and feedback.

Indeed, dealing with an unfamiliar department culture, new (and more senior) colleagues, and a distinct university bureaucracy is just the beginning of what is often an unsettling experience. New faculty members are also faced with the task of balancing their time and prioritizing their obligations. Professionally this may include multiple new course preparations, expectations for external grant procurement, research and publishing, as well as an influx of student mentoring/advising and an obligation of service/committee work. There are a myriad of personal adjustments as well, including long-distance moves, new housing, and relationship management with partners, spouses, family, and friends, all of which complicate maintaining a balanced and healthy lifestyle. Women, in particular, often face heightened struggles with managing work responsibilities alongside family obligations, especially those involving children.

Current state of academe and concerns of new faculty

The economic downturn of recent years has affected the climate of higher education in several ways. One primary change has been a shrinking pool of new tenure-track faculty appointments, as compared to various contingent (nontenure-track) positions (Monks 2009). Nationally, nontenure-track appointments now account for 65 percent of the faculty in degree-granting institutions (Bradley 2005). Such changes are occurring under the auspices of fiscal savings (Sorcinelli 2007), and include lower pay, few if any fringe benefits, and short-term contracts that make such appointments attractive to institutional administrators. For those who have accepted contingent positions, there is concern about how such appointments place them on an endless cycle of shoelacing unpredictable and temporary jobs (Adams 2002). Finishing your degree and/or publishing are extremely difficult under such circumstances, though often necessary for career advancement. Moreover, such appointments are traditionally looked down upon by the academic bourgeoisie.

Connected to this is a trend toward expanding faculty roles for both tenure and nontenure-track positions. Faculty are being increasingly expected to do more (teaching, research, and service) with the same or fewer resources (Sorcinelli 2007). Standards for retention (a.k.a. annual, pretenure or reappointment reviews), tenure, and promotion benchmarks thus seem to be rising, demanding faculty fluently play "jack of all trades." It is indeed no surprise then that academe has taken on a more competitive and less cooperative character, with success being more product-oriented than human-oriented (Risden 1995).

For new PhDs, cuts in higher education and the increasing scarcity of secure, long-term academic appointments translate into feelings of employment desperation. Many are faced with accepting positions whenever and wherever they can get them. The environments of such places may be quite different from those characterizing graduate school (Adams 2002; Austin 2002; Boice 1993). While most doctoral programs are housed within research-intensive universities, the majority of graduate students find positions in other types of institutions, often with higher expectations for teaching and service. Indeed, the primary responsibilities within such institutions are more along the lines of general education, with faculty members being expected to work as generalists, teaching across an array of topics, managing several sections of introductory courses, and even offering remedial courses. Such teaching responsibilities are balanced with various time-intensive service tasks related to academic advising, employment/ career coaching, and personal counseling. An active research agenda may not even be expected in such institutions (Adams 2002).

Complicating the work of faculty in many of today's universities and colleges are various pedagogical challenges related to the contemporary student body (Wulff and Austin 2004). Particularly noteworthy is a report by the Association of American Colleges and Universities (Adams 2002) which found over half of entering students are academically unprepared (lacking reading, writing and/or math skills). Such scenarios often cause a disjuncture between faculty expectations and student capabilities (Sorcinelli 2007). This might be a particular challenge for you as a new faculty who might not have substantial classroom experience, having perhaps only your own (often quite successful) experiences or most recent (graduate) coursework to reflect upon, both of which are not likely to offer much assistance in working with undergraduate students of varying abilities. In related fashion, as contemporary student bodies become more accustomed to various sorts of technologies used for instruction (Wulff and Austin 2004) and a more diverse student body in terms of gender, race, ethnicity, class, age, religion/spirituality, sexual identity, and orientation, (Sorcinelli 2007; Wulff and Austin 2004), teaching and service responsibilities will only become increasingly challenging (Adams 2002).

It is not surprising, then, that you are frequently overwhelmed by the type and volume of work expected of you (Adams 2002). Part of the problem is graduate students, in general, do not seem to enter academic posts with the preparation, knowledge, and information necessary to quickly and effectively adjust to their new positions (Adams 2002; French 2006). Training within primarily research-intensive universities has not included preparation for understanding the vast array of institutions where graduates are likely to be employed (Adams 2002). This can leave one feeling isolated, alienated, lonely, confused, and disenchanted (Boice 1993, 2000). What many do not know is such feelings are shared by most others (Boice 1993; Lucas and Murry 2002; Price et al. 2002). Only an estimated 2–3 percent of new faculty are ahead of this learning curve from the start (Boice 2000).

What seems to be of foremost concern to new faculty is the vagueness with which expectations and standards for their work are communicated (Boice 1993, 2000). While orientations may be offered, these are often university/college-wide events and thus center on more generic and abstract content. Matters of most immediate and pragmatic concern to new faculty (i.e., parking, office equipment, book orders, class rosters, audiovisual needs) are often informally contingent on the availability and helpfulness of department staff (Price et al. 2002). Meanwhile, matters of greatest salience to a new faculty's future (standards of retention, tenure, and/or promotion) are often relegated to ambiguously written statements and conversations with department chairs and more senior colleagues. Given that different people may have distinct interpretations and perspectives on these standards, new faculty sometimes feel as though their colleagues are purposely withholding imperative information, leading them to conclude that their coworkers are either apathetic, lack collegiality, or are even outright antagonistic (Adams 2002; Boice 1993, 2000). Of course this is not often the case, but for a new faculty with little contextual or institutional history and knowledge to draw upon there may be few alternative conclusions.

While it is of course important for a person to gather information about a place prior to interviewing or accepting a job offer there, as discussed in Chapter 2 (Vesilind 2000), it is not always possible to obtain as complete a set of information, nor a true "feel" for the climate and environment until one is at the institution, if even then (Rosser 2003). Given you may have been told during interviews, orientations, in written documents and informal conversations that faculty development is a priority of an institution, and indeed understand that your "development" in the areas of teaching, service, and research may very well seal your fate at a particular university or college, it seems at the least contradictory that expectations for retention, tenure, and promotion continue to be notoriously vague (Vesilind 2000). Such ambiguity works to produce a constant fear that whatever you do/produce will not be sufficient for a continued contract and/or tenure (Adams 2002). It is no wonder so many begin to feel disconnected from their institutions within the first few months (or perhaps years) of employment. It is certainly difficult to commit to a place where one has felt little investment in return (Boice 1993).

Being unsure of exactly what you ought to be doing, you may focus on preparing your classes, as such a task requires immediate attention and, at least for those with teaching experience, this also provides a much needed sense of structure and purpose (Boice 1993). Indicative of this is the finding by Angelo and Cross (1993) that an estimated 70 percent of faculty are more interested in teaching than other professional activities. This statistic sheds important light on the mindset of new faculty, as most are concerned about the number and range of new classes they are to teach (Boice 1993). Unfortunately, however, you may spend too much time on teaching and end up feeling as though you have little energy left over for other professional obligations, such as research (Adams 2002). A diversion from working on research may be welcome for a while, since many new faculty are also not well versed in the world of academic publishing (Boice 2000; Silverman 1999) and often experience writer's block as a result (Boice 1993, 2000). However, such avoidance only fuels a sense of dread with the confusion over vague productivity standards.

Additional time management concerns occur over the balance of one's professional and personal life (French 2006). While most new faculty are willing to work hard within their new academic positions, you also face important, time-consuming and stressful personal transitions and need to balance such demands alongside your professional roles (Wieck 2003). For example, your family may have trouble adjusting to a new community, job, and/or school. Moreover, finding appropriate housing, unpacking, and settling into a new community is likely to be nerve-racking (Price et al. 2002). Many worry devoting much time or energy to their personal lives will distract them from professional obligations, especially the time and energy crunch surrounding the development of one's research agenda (Boice 2000). Finding this balance is among other issues related to being a new female faculty member and can be especially problematic for women.

Issues for women

Women continue to be underrepresented in academe, particularly at the highest ranks, and those who do enter the professional academic world may be subjected to a host of sexist attitudes and practices (Dallimore 2003; Dominici et al. 2009). This can be manifested in several ways related to the professional–personal balance. It is worth underscoring that this and many other concerns may often aptly apply to persons of color, nonheterosexual orientation, and/or those with disabilities.

Being new faculty, as well as a deviation from the (male) norm, may illicit seemingly innocent inquiries by your colleagues and support staff that may appear rude, intrusive, or sexist. For example, as Darlington and Durnell (1996) have noted with regard to being a racial minority, new faculty might find that interest is expressed by their coworkers about their personal lives. Speaking specifically of gender, Dallimore (2003) found, though illegal, such inquiries often begin during the interviewing process. Who does she live with? Is she married? Is she dating? Does she have kids? Will she one day? While some of this may simply be due to the novelty of having a woman in a male-dominated profession and/or department, such questions can easily carry disparaging overtones when the message portrayed is one of women being more concerned about their personal lives than their professional endeavors. Indeed, Dallimore (2003) found female faculty experience such inquiries much more often than male faculty. Such exchanges may weigh heavily in the early socialization experiences of new academics, particularly in their perceptions of the institutions that hired them and their role within those institutions. This is especially true when more formal means of orientation and preparation are lacking (Dallimore 2003).

In related fashion, you may struggle with how to present your family, should you have a partner and/or children, to your colleagues. In a classic work on women in academe, Caplan (1993) discussed the "maleness" of academe, and subsequent frustrations and challenges posed to women. Traditionally, male academics have not been expected to assume the majority or even their share of domestic responsibilities; most were either bachelors or had trailing spouses who assumed such roles. This trend, incidentally, continues. Male academics are more likely than female academics to have spouses and children. In fact, having a family increases the likelihood of career advancement for men (Dominici et al. 2009). The opposite is true for women academics. In some disciplines women are actually twice as likely as men to be single and are less likely to advance up the academic ladder if they have, particularly young, children (Dominici et al. 2009). Moreover, women are much more likely than men to recognize the struggle of balancing family and professional responsibilities, suggesting that it is still the case that many men are not thusly burdened (Dallimore 2003). Such differences do indeed affect the success rates of traditionally ranked faculty, as men are 20 percent more likely than women to receive tenure annually (Mason et al. 2006).

Revisiting the issue of economics and trends in the profession as they relate to women is informative. As discussed in Chapter 3, the earning gap persists in academe. For our purposes, it is helpful to note that, on the whole, women make 81 percent of what men make across rank (assistant, associate, and full professor), type of institution (public, private independent, or religious), and level of degree granted at the institution (doctoral, master's, baccalaureate, and associate) (West and Curtis 2006). Moreover, women are underrepresented across tenure-track and tenured appointments, but overrepresented among contingent positions. While women make up half (50.1 percent) of doctoral recipients, they account for 54 percent of instructors and lecturers, 47 percent of assistant professors, 40 percent of associate professors, and 26 percent of full professors (U.S. Department of Education 2009).

Thus, the traditional notion that new tenure-track faculty (and those striving to attain such a position) ought to devote nearly every living moment to academe is easily perpetuated. The American Sociological Association (2000) found more than 40 percent of new assistant professors put in over fifty hours per week. Even the mere thought of what will be expected of them can drive women who have or hope to have families out of the academic pipeline. Not only does it becomes obvious to many that their biological clocks coincide with their tenure clocks, but the time demands of the profession seem to conflict too greatly with the time demands of raising a family (Dominici et al. 2009; Sorcinelli 2007). Women are thus forced to make difficult decisions about their professional and personal lives, and many do so before even attempting to enter the more lucrative (compared to contingent positions) and stable (over the long term) arena of tenure-track appointments (Dominici et al. 2009). Understandably then, new female faculty may hesitate to share much about their personal lives for fear that it will cause them to look like less serious or committed scholars. It is well understood that personal sacrifices are necessary in order to succeed along a traditional academic path, and not mentioning your personal obligations may be one of them (Dallimore 2003).

However, family and childbearing/raising issues are just part of the picture, as the problem is not exclusively one of women opting out. Another aspect of being a new female faculty member is the social, intellectual, and political isolation you may feel when you enter an environment that has traditionally excluded you and marginalized your concerns (Boice 1993). Today, few departments are able to hire more than one faculty a year, and even this has become a luxury at many institutions. Thus, women may arrive at their departments as the only new hire, and find they are closer in age and experience to the students in their class than they are to their own colleagues (Adams 2002). Not only might your interests and views not be representative of the majority within your department, you might also sense a complete lack of commonality and community with your colleagues on whom you are to rely for mentorship and guidance, not to mention retention, tenure, and promotion. Research has confirmed new female faculty often have trouble identifying appropriate mentors and/or building professional networks, especially including other women who have successfully traversed the academic landscape (Dallimore 2003).

While procedures vary, it remains a widely held belief, and practice in some cases, that decisions regarding retention, tenure, and promotion are made subjectively based on whether a person is well liked and seen as a good colleague, as opposed to a more objective set of criteria for productivity (Boice 2000; Price et al. 2002). Women who feel isolated from their departments may suffer stress and anxiety as a result of subjectivity that allows for sexist influences on decisions.

Another aspect of being a new female faculty member that feeds into sexism is the way in which being seen as distinct from others may subject a person to extra (or specific) tasks (Dallimore 2003; Price et al. 2002). Just as patriarchal attitudes within academe subject women to the stereotype of caring more about their personal lives than their professional responsibilities, so too might they be subjected to gendered expectations with regard to particular types of service efforts. For example, you may be seen as more social and thus relied upon to organize events like annual banquets or award receptions. In this vein, you may be seen as more emotionally connected to your students and thus better to slate as counselors and advisors (Adams 2002). This can occur from the opposite direction as well, with students feeling more comfortable coming to female faculty about their concerns, and exhibiting greater informality in doing so (Dallimore 2003). Such scenarios easily translate to greater student advisees in general, or all advisees of a particular demographic (in this case, likely based on gender) (Adams 2002). The fact that many women believe they must outperform their male counterparts in order to earn equitable respect only complicates the matter of disparate service obligations (Dallimore 2003).

The issue of having to produce more than men and sexist stereotyping may translate into the classroom context as well, where gendered differences in student evaluations have been well documented (see Massoni 2004 for a review). For instance, female professors are typically seen as more caring than male professors (Bachen et al. 1999; Sprague and Massoni 2002). They are subsequently expected to be, and often become, more actively nurturing and available for consultations and meetings. By comparison, male professors who are noted for being caring seem to make the mark for simply expressing concern for their students (Basow 2000; Bennet 1982; Sprague and Massoni 2002). Male professors also seem to benefit from being perceived as more knowledgeable, objective, prepared, and professional as compared to female professors (Bachen et al. 1999; Basow 1995; Centra and Gaubatz 2000). For new faculty who happen to appear or be relatively young, the combination of gender and age compounds the problem, as students seem to take greater liberties in their expectations of, communication with and respect for young female faculty (Dallimore 2003).

Survival strategies

Acclimation

One key to acclimating to the new institution, job, students, and colleagues is to know something about what you are getting into. It is generally understood that as difficult and time-consuming as the task may be, it is absolutely necessary to familiarize yourself with the climate and culture of your new institution and department. This includes understanding the institution's mission and the subsequent expectations for teaching, research, and service. This should be an ongoing process, both prior and subsequent to accepting a position.

Advanced graduate students and new faculty are advised to consult the Carnegie Foundation classifications (2009), as these can provide a helpful rubric for categorizing institutions. Additionally, applicants and new faculty should obtain any and all materials related to the institution's mission and expectations of faculty at the department, college, and university levels. These materials may take various forms, like a faculty handbook, orientation pamphlet, retention, tenure and promotion guidelines, or faculty union contract. Useful information may be found in more than one source, so do not stop the search after finding a single document. Such materials can be helpful in formulating questions and discussion points in preparation for meetings with your department/unit chair/director, other administrators (e.g., dean, associate dean, provost, union officers) and senior colleagues. Taking the initiative to schedule such appointments in advance (perhaps even on an annual basis) not only helps you become accustomed to your surroundings, it also presents a positive and proactive persona to those whose opinions will be of consequence in the future. It might be possible to expand the nature of these meetings to be somewhat social as well, perhaps going to coffee or lunch with each individual. If such opportunities come to fruition, make a point of asking each person a little more about her/himself. Most academics love an opportunity to talk about themselves and their work. Requesting a copy of the person's curriculum vitae can also be an additional resource in determining what the expectations of faculty are.

However, a note of caution here. Do not expect such meetings to be easy to schedule. Your colleagues, if they are inclined to approach new faculty at all, are likely to do so early on. As a semester or year progresses, schedules become tight. Scheduling meetings early in the semester/year and exercising patience in doing so will be of great benefit. Moreover, prepare to hear ambiguous answers by many in terms of what is expected of new faculty regarding retention, tenure, and promotion. Strict guides, such as the exact number of publications necessary, may not be a matter of written policy, and, depending on how active and senior the colleagues are, they may be out of touch about contemporary standards. Also note even if something concrete is written in some guideline, recent norms and practices may be different. People who went before you may have set the bar higher than that which is formally stated. It is a wise idea to avoid being a marginal or barely acceptable retention, tenure, or promotion case. If you fear any discrimination or lack of collegiality, surpassing minimum standards can provide you with an important safety net, as well as grounds for a grievance, appeal, or lawsuit, if necessary. If specific details are unavailable or vague, try to at least glean a basic understanding of what is expected by different colleagues. For example, you could ask how the areas of teaching, research, and service are weighted (perhaps ask for a percentage breakdown – i.e., 40 percent on teaching, 30 percent on research, and 30 percent on service). Such guides can be very helpful in planning your time and working agenda.

A simple way of thinking about this is that if your retention, tenure, and promotion materials regarding teaching will be weighted 40 percent, plan your workweek such that you spend 40 percent of your time on instructional tasks, and so on. This can be quite helpful in preserving some of your time for personal hobbies and family obligations as well.

Establishing mentoring relationships outside your department or unit can be quite advantageous, particularly if meeting with your immediate supervisor or other senior colleagues is not possible or comfortable. One strategy is to locate senior faculty in other departments with whom you might have something in common (e.g., research and teaching interests, demographic). Such people are in a unique position of being outside of your immediate department or unit but within the university, so they can offer a helpful insider–outsider perspective on climate and expectations. Again a bit of caution is merited. It is politically astute to listen more and talk less (ask questions rather than take hard stances, especially on controversial issues or on particular individuals) until gaining a bit more familiarity with the environment of the university. It could be devastating to inadvertently insult a potential ally and confidant because one is unfamiliar with the history between departments, people, and issues/policies. If political land mines seem rampant at your institution, a safer route may be to try to establish such relationships within the professional networks available at academic conferences. Conferences can also be helpful for establishing a peer network, if your institution has not done much hiring in recent years or you find little in common with other new hires. Even if people are from different institutions, comparing experiences, lending support, and establishing a type of comentoring system (see McGuire and Reger 2003) can be very helpful in warding off feelings of isolation and anxiety.

A few other pieces of advice bear mentioning with regard to initially acclimating to a job. First, respect and, if desirable, befriend office support staff. They hold more power than they are given credit for and can make things happen for you under the radar (e.g., expediting travel requests, ordering particular office supplies, securing an extra filing cabinet). Second, make a point of spending a few extra hours each week in your office, just for visibility's sake. Not only might there be unwritten rules about how many hours a week faculty should be around beyond regularly scheduled office hours, but such visibility and accessibility is often the only way for your colleagues to gauge your productivity within the early months of your employment (Price et al. 2002). If you prefer to do most of your work at home, plan your office time around the hours when most colleagues are also around, so as to get the most from your effort.

Teaching

Acclimating to a new job often revolves around preparations for classes and interactions with students. This is because there is probably nothing else within your new job that demands as much immediate attention and provides as much structure and constant feedback (as opposed to service- and research-related tasks, where expectations can seem ambiguous). The problem comes when new faculty spend too much time on their teaching duties, proportionately to other tasks. The simple rule provided earlier about corresponding the weight given to teaching to the time devoted to it weekly can be helpful. This may be particularly important if you are in a teaching-intensive university or college and/or on a contingent appointment hoping to remain marketable for other positions. A few additional points may also help put teaching into perspective.

First, realize you are indeed smarter than the students in your classes. This is not an insult to your students; it is recognition that you have spent a great deal more time studying the topics than they have. Second, accept the likelihood that the average undergraduate student might not recognize the difference between a lecture that took you two hours to prepare and one that took eight. You know more than you might think you do; you need not read everything ever written on a topic before feeling competent to talk about it. As women, we are often quick to downplay the level of our intellect and skill. This has been referred to as the "imposter syndrome" within the DWC workshops. You suffer from imposter syndrome each time you question your knowledge and talent, followed by the assumption that it was a fluke that you were offered your position and that someone will eventually figure you to be a fraud. Try not to let such self-defeatism get the best of you. Instead, try to figure out the line between perfect and solid preparation. Keep Boice's (2000) concept of "nihil nimius" (nothing in excess – everything in moderation) in mind.

Third, recognize that a very common trap for new instructors is to cover too much within a class period as well as over the course of a semester. Pick and choose the most important material and leave the rest for assigned reading (you may always give a quiz or quick essay at the beginning of the next class session), independent studies, advanced seminars, or graduate classes. If you are not sure about what to cut, take the opportunity during any meetings you arrange with colleagues to ask for their input. Also, request copies of past syllabuses, textbooks, and other materials from them or the office staff. True, your courses may have already begun by the time you are able to do this, but recognize it often takes about three runs at a course before really getting it down. Just consider the initial semester a test case of sorts. You do not need to reinvent the wheel every time you teach a class. Give yourself a chance to repeat the parts of a course you like and tweak the parts you do not. Within your retention, tenure, and promotion dossier, you can simply talk about how your teaching evolved and your pedagogical repertoire expanded over subsequent semesters. Remember that offering a smooth and successful course comes with time and practice and can be an amazing confidence booster.

A few additional suggestions may help female faculty, in particular, adjust to their teaching obligations. It is important to recognize that you are seen in many roles by your students (e.g., instructor, counselor, ally, advocate, confidant, friend, big sister/aunt/mother). While this often allows us to find more meaning in our work, it can also be a source of strain, frustration, and confusion when we experience role conflict. Given the literature cited earlier regarding tokenism and the ways in which female faculty may be exploited in terms of our work with students, it might be helpful to plan ahead for how you will handle such matters, keeping in mind both your emotional and ethical/legal boundaries. For instance, if a student comes to you with a complaint of harassment by another student, it is not appropriate for you to try to handle the situation alone. There are often policies for handling such matters as well as university personnel who have been trained to handle these situations. Additionally, bear in mind that your department chair and senior colleagues can be your greatest resource and allies in situations like that.

Also, try to prepare for the potential time students will request of you outside of class. Setting aside certain days for teaching/course management and others for research/writing can be wise. Keep phone calls, emails, meetings, and so on restricted to the teaching days. Let your students know when they can expect responses from you, especially for email, at the beginning of the semester. You may even want to consider including such information as a section in your course syllabus. While it might feel validating to connect with students, the more you do so, the more emotional energy and time will be spent within your instructional/advising capacity. Price et al. (2002) have several more specific strategies for managing student contact. The point is that maintaining some professional distance is important for both you and your students, and imperative to the balancing act you face within a new academic appointment.

In related fashion, you may want to prepare ahead of time for how you will set up levels of credibility and formality with students – anything from making clear how you expect to be addressed, to guidelines on how to write a professional email. Collect any reports, studies, or other documentation that attest to gendered differences in student evaluations and file them in your retention, tenure, and promotion file if you suspect this might be an issue. At the end of the semester (or around graduation time if you have had them in several of your classes) students may send you emails and cards thanking you for your time and efforts. Save all of these and include them in your retention, tenure, and promotion file. Such unsolicited documentation may buffer negative comments on course evaluations. Moreover, if you should come across any agitated or aggressive students who want to meet with you, particularly those of the opposite sex, do not do so behind closed doors. If a confrontation is anticipated, have another person in the room (or at least within earshot) and consult your immediate supervisor and/or department chair in advance, if possible. As a general rule, consider always having your office door open during office hours as well. Such issues are a matter of protecting your personal safety and professional reputation.

Research

Some form of research or scholarship is usually a part of every new faculty member's job. Just as with minding the weight given to teaching, it is imperative to understand the weight *and* nature of scholarship required at your particular institution, as new faculty are expected to develop a research agenda that conforms to such standards. On one end of this spectrum, you may be required to incorporate recent research into your curriculum or attend a conference a couple of times before tenure review. On the other end, you may need to publish two or more peer-reviewed articles within particular journals each year and secure a certain amount of research funding. An easy mistake to make is to assume that the definition of research and scholarship at your doctoral institution is the same as that at your new place of employment. Most doctoral programs are housed within research-centered universities and most of us do not secure positions at such institutions. Along with the various meetings and information searches you do as part of acclimating to your new job, keep an eye toward uncovering the resources available for research as well. Be aware that you may not have access to as updated or expansive libraries, software, and internal seed money. You may also be expected to engage undergraduates in research, as opposed to hiring graduate assistants or conducting solo-based research.

It is within the research realm that procrastination and distraction are probably most salient within the first few months (or years) of an academic appointment. Be prepared that the first semester may not allow you much time for research and writing. Acclimation and teaching tasks will be very time-consuming, so try to make use of weekends, holidays, and semester breaks. It will be increasingly difficult to get your mind back on research and writing the longer you wait (recall how "breaks" disrupted your dissertation progress). A couple of strategies may help. One is to do a little every day. You might be surprised at how much you can accomplish with just an hour or even half-hour devoted to writing, so long as the time is actually devoted to writing, not checking emails, messaging on Facebook, etc. The second is to spend intense amounts of time over holidays, long weekends, or slow class weeks. Again, it can be surprising how much may be accomplished during times of little interruption. You will likely find your work style, personality, and family obligations fit one or the other strategy best. Regardless, set goals for this work, on a yearly, semester, monthly, weekly, or even daily basis. Sometimes a little micromanagement of the self can make the difference between progress and stagnation.

Also be aware that it is extremely easy to be wooed into all sorts of new projects when really your most efficient strategy is to make use of your dissertation for at least a few publications. It may seem like everyone in your new department wants to involve you in something, which can feel very good. Selecting minor roles in a few particularly interesting projects can be a wise idea, because such efforts make you appear like a team player. However, there really is not time to take a lead on many, if any, new projects. Tenure may seem like a long time away, but time sneaks up and slips by quickly. Moreover, keep in mind that your progress will likely be formally gauged through retention and pretenure reviews, so you must show productivity early on. As we mentioned earlier, at some institutions the number of publications is often unclear for tenure. You might want to keep tabs on who is going up for tenure and what they have done. At the end of the day, it will not matter how many projects you participated in if nothing was ever published. Also keep in mind that book reviews, op-eds, newsletters, etc. are not substitutes for peer review articles and book chapters.

Also be reasonable about your expectations for grant procurement, should it be a priority at your university. Large federal grants are usually awarded to well-seasoned (and connected) researchers and their project teams. Invitations to become members of such teams can help lay the groundwork for future funding, and are one of the few occasions when it is worth considering a new project within the first few years. However, you are not likely to be awarded substantial grants on your own merit this early, and putting together applications for them can be as time-consuming as preparing an article manuscript. If lip service to grants is important, work on internal "seed" grants and smaller, local, foundation-based funding sources. It is surprising how quickly several small awards add up.

If you are having trouble figuring out where to submit your work, consultations with your peers and senior colleagues, both within and outside your department and university, can be helpful. Depending upon your interests and the type of research you do, there may be more or fewer outlets – more for quantitative work using traditional theory, fewer for qualitative work using feminist, radical, or fringe theory. If you are in the latter camp, make good use of the handful of outlets available to you. In order to broaden the diversity of your publications, watch for special issues in journals that you might not regularly consider and make use of almost every publishing opportunity. Listservs, for example, can be tremendous sources for learning about anthologies in progress and calls for papers. Do not wait for a paper to be perfect. If it is good enough to strike a reviewer's or editor's interest, you will likely be given an opportunity to revise and resubmit. Never turn such opportunities down, especially if it is because of the criticism you received on the first draft (unless it would substantially alter the paper in a way that does not feel right to you). It is important to take criticism with a grain of salt; it is simply part of the process. Finally, do not be dissuaded by a rejection at a particular journal. Much of the publishing game is about finding the right fit for your piece. If you feel good about your work and believe it is publishable, keep sending it out to other outlets. The same paper may be rejected several times before being accepted somewhere.

A couple of additional points regarding the handling of your scholarship are worth noting. First, when writing about your research in your retention, tenure, and promotion dossier, resist the urge to refer to your graduate work. This can be quite tempting in terms of discussing your dissertation research, but you must now play the part of a faculty member (even if you do not yet feel the part). In a first- or second-year review, reflections on the work produced from your dissertation may be appropriate. However, you must eventually show

yond this work, even if you are still reanalyzing the same data (which
egitimate to do). A simple strategy is to talk in terms of your "research
and how your work is evolving in different, yet related, directions.
ᴐimply avoiding the word "dissertation" can be all it takes to portray yourself
as an independent and evolving scholar. Second, if time is tight and teaching
commitments are high, remember that teaching in itself can also be an area of
scholarship, research, and publication. Several journals address and/or specia-
lize in publishing work on pedagogical advances, curriculum development, use
of technology, and the like. Third, if you are unsure about staying at your
current place of employment, or otherwise just want to keep your options open,
think ahead of what might be required at the types of institutions where you
may like to work one day. The degree and nature of your scholarship often
either open or close these doors. You do not need to know the exact university
you might want to move to, but rather the *type* of university (e.g., community
college, small liberal arts and/or faith-based college, comprehensive university,
research university). In short, research, write, and publish according to where
you want to be in the future, as opposed to where you are at the moment.

Service

While many new faculty today have been exposed to some aspects of
teaching and research during graduate school, service may be a foreign concept.
Thankfully, sometimes new faculty are not expected to participate in much
committee work during their first semester, or even their first year. However, at
some point, most do need to devote at least some of their time to service-related
tasks, as such work counts toward retention, tenure, and promotion, albeit to
varying degrees. Putting a little time into understanding these expectations, as
well as what types of assignments are available, can be helpful in avoiding
exploitive and undesirable responsibilities. Once expectations and options are
understood, diplomacy and selectivity are key. Some service-related assignments
are relatively benign and require only a few hours a year (e.g., library acquisi-
tions committee), while others are politically laden and require several hours a
month or week (e.g., hiring committee).

While standards vary, it is generally advisable to keep service in check, as it
can be very easy to end up on several administrative and student committees.
This only pulls you away from teaching and research, both of which are often
weighted more heavily. One strategy for managing service is to volunteer for a
couple of assignments, rather than wait to be assigned. Doing so not only
allows you to select the assignments that feel most meaningful, it also shows
initiative and interest in your department or unit. Note that most service-related
responsibilities occur at this level, although it might be wise to volunteer for
one or two committees at higher levels (within your college or university) prior
to final tenure review. Such experience broadens the diversity of your work and
exposes you to colleagues and administrators outside of your department,
which can be refreshing and politically astute.

Service can also take the form of assuming tasks within professional academic organizations and within community groups. While such endeavors can be important networking opportunities, they too can easily consume your time and energy. Additionally, in many institutions they are considered less important than department, college, and university-based service. This is particularly true of community-based activism, which may seem nonsensical if you entered higher education with an eye toward public intellectualism and social justice. Rely upon the strategies outlined under "Acclimation" to understand in advance what the attitude of such work is within your department. If you are unsure, tread lightly in terms of sharing your pursuits with your colleagues until you have a firmer sense of departmental culture. Such activities may be read as either nice but not relevant, or an extravagance, and an indication that your university-based duties are either not numerous enough or not being taken seriously enough. Look at Few et al. (2007) for a thought-provoking essay on the matter of redefining scholarship and activism while on the tenure track.

A couple of additional caveats bear mentioning. Beware of the potential, as discussed earlier, for exploitation based on how your colleagues perceive you. If you are a minority in any way, be it by gender, race, ethnicity, age, sexual orientation, etc., you may find you are expected to assume more service or particular types of service. While such work might be the most meaningful to you (i.e., being a member of the women's caucus, advising a feminist-based undergraduate club), it is ultimately unfair and discriminatory for you to be expected to do more because of your status or demographic. Using some simple negotiation strategies can eliminate other responsibilities from your plate so you can devote time to such activities (e.g., "I would really enjoy serving on the women's caucus, but I am very busy with the curriculum committee right now. Who could take my place there, so that I can become involved with the caucus?").

Note that exploitation can also occur because of your diligence in doing a good and responsible job at your service tasks. While excelling in this arena may help establish you as an upstanding, committed colleague, also know that not everyone puts in this type of effort, and administrators tend to increasingly rely on those who have shown capacity to handle their obligations. It is thus possible to end up with more than your fair share of work because of your commitment to getting the job done. This is not to suggest a lackadaisical attitude toward service. However, it is advisable to know what the standards are for service work and to compare what you are doing with others, to the extent you are able.

Balancing professional and personal

While several suggestions with regard to time management and balance have already been provided within the earlier sections of this chapter, a few additional points are worth noting. First, given the potential for sexist stereotyping of female faculty, you may want to keep your personal affairs relatively private around the office, at least for the first few months until you can glean a feel for the appropriateness of discussing such matters openly within your department. If/when asked, short and positive responses may be the safest avenue. However, recognize that there may come a time when your personal and professional lives will merge, such as at a department reception or banquet, and anticipate how comfortable you are with exposing aspects of your personal life in such cases.

On the other hand, be cognizant of times when divulging more about your personal life is necessary. For example, if you are being called away to tend to a family member who has fallen ill and miss several of your classes and other meetings as a result, it is important to let your immediate supervisor and/or chair know, as opposed to trying to cover the matter up or handle it informally yourself (e.g., having your teaching assistant cover several lectures). It would be much better to have this information come from you directly than to risk it getting back to your colleagues through student complaints or inquiries about why you are never in your office or at faculty meetings, etc.

While distancing your personal life while at work may be helpful, it is not necessarily desirable to do the same thing in reverse. It is important to help loved ones know and understand the nature of your work and the pressure you are under. This may not necessarily need to be dinner conversation. In fact, you may consciously choose not to share work-related issues on a regular basis at home. However, these people may be your sole source of support within the first few years. Regardless of how stressful the move was, they love you and they want to support you. Let them.

Finally, regardless of what is happening at your new job, it is important to your mental stability to get a life, literally, outside of the institution. This may involve time with your loved ones, or devotion to your favorite hobby (perhaps actually finding a hobby). Such matters may, and possibly should, remain separate from your professional work and contacts (recall the traditional thinking that nothing but work exists while on the tenure track). Regardless, having something to distract you and provide a release from the stress of your professional life will not only aid your health and well-being, it may likely help you become more professionally productive.

Conclusion

We have only been able to cover some of the recurrent themes here. What is clear from both the literature reviewed in the first half of this chapter, and the advice shared in the second, is that new faculty members often feel pulled in multiple directions, struggling to adjust and balance their new roles. They may consequently become overwhelmed, overburdened, stressed out, isolated, confused, and disenchanted. While the mentoring and guidance of supervisors, administrators, and other faculty members can help in this transition, not all new professors have or are able to develop such relationships. Frustration may be further complicated by instances in which new academics have found themselves in contingent positions, yet hope to move on to more permanent and/or tenure-track appointments. For those within tenure-track appointments, it may be quite demoralizing to have made concerted attempts to research a university, department, and community before accepting their position, and yet still find themselves in unsupportive environments or working under unclear expectations. Sadly this is too often connected to institutional and interpersonal forms of sexism.

Our hope with this chapter was to offer a variety of suggestions, points of consideration, and strategies to new academics who have opted to enter the professional academic world. Of course, it would be helpful if calls for institutional reform with regard to the preparation of graduate students and the socialization of new faculty were to be taken seriously (see Adams 2002, Dallimore 2003, French 2006, Hessler and Ritchie 2006, and Sorcinelli 2007 for programming suggestions). The Preparing Future Faculty (PFF) program (2009) has made significant strides in this direction, but many doctorate-granting institutions have yet to explore its potential. In the meantime, the DWC has and remains committed to helping new scholars with this particular rite of passage. Professional academe can be a very stressful occupation; however, it may also be a very honorable, satisfying, and comparatively stable one. It is important for those of us who have successfully navigated its waters to assist others, such that the "prospect of surviving in academe may seem less mysterious and more manageable" (Boice 1993: 253).

References

Adams, K. A. (2002) *What Colleges and Universities Want in New Faculty*, Washington, DC: Association of American Colleges and Universities.

American Sociological Association (2000) *New Doctorates in Sociology: Professions Inside and Outside the Academy*, Washington, DC: American Sociological Association.

Angelo, T. A., and Cross, K. P. (1993) *Classroom Assessment Techniques: A Handbook for College Teachers*, 2nd edn, San Francisco,CA: Jossey-Bass.

Austin, A. E. (2002) "Preparing the next generation: graduate school as socialization to the academic career," *Journal of Higher Education*, 73: 94–122.

Bachen, C., McLoughlin, M., and Garcia, S. (1999) "Assessing the role of gender in college students' evaluations of faculty," *Communication Education*, 48: 193–210.

Basow, S. A. (1995) "Student evaluation of college professors: when gender matters," *Journal of Educational Psychology*, 87 (4): 656–65.

Basow, S. A. (2000) "Best and worst professors: gender patterns in students' choices," *Sex Roles*, 3 (5–6): 401–17.

Bennet, S. K. (1982) "Student perceptions of and expectations for male and female instructors: evidence relating to the question of gender bias in teaching evaluation," *Journal of Educational Psychology*, 74 (2): 170–79.

Boice, R. (1993) *The New Faculty Member: Supporting and Fostering Professional Development*, San Francisco,CA Jossey-Bass.

Boice, R. (2000) *Advice for New Faculty Members: Nihil Nimius*, Needham Heights, MA: Allyn & Bacon.

Bradley, G. (2005) "Proportion on tenure track drops," *Academe*, 91 (4): 5.

Caplan, P. J. (1993) *Lifting a Ton of Feathers: A Woman's Guide to Surviving in the Academic World*, Toronto, Ont.: University of Toronto Press.

Carnegie Foundation for the Advancement of Teaching (2009) *The Carnegie Classification of Institutions of Higher Education*, Stanford, CA: Carnegie Foundation. Online. Available http: http://www.carnegiefoundation.org/classifications/ (accessed July 30, 2009).

Centra, J., and Gaubatz, N. (2000) "Is there gender bias in student evaluations of teaching?," *Journal of Higher Education*, 71: 17–33.

Dallimore, E. J. (2003) "Memorable messages as discursive formations: the gendered socialization of new university faculty," *Women's Studies in Communication*, 26 (2): 214–65.

Darlington, P. S. E., and Durnell, N. Y. (1996) "The last word. Faculty life 101: a survival guide," *Black Issues in Higher Education*, 13 (26): 112.

Dominici, F., Fried, L. P., and Zeger, S. L. (2009) "So few women leaders," *Academe*, 95 (4): 25–27.

Few, A. L., Piercy, F. P., and Stremmel, A. (2007) "Balancing the passion for activism with the demands of tenure: one professional's story from three perspectives," *NWSA Journal*, 19 (3): 47–66.

French, D. P. (2006) "What they don't know," *Journal of College Science Teaching*, 35 (7): 62–63.

Hessler, K., and Ritchie, H. (2006) "Faculty forum: recruitment and retention of novice faculty," *Journal of Nursing Education*, 45 (5): 150–54.

Lucas, C. J., and Murry, J. W. (2002) *New Faculty: A Practical Guide for Academic Beginners*, New York: Palgrave.

McGuire, G. M., and Reger, J. (2003) "Feminist co-mentoring: a model for academic professional development," *NWSA Journal*, 15 (1): 54–70.

Mason, M. A., Goulden, M., and Wolfinger, N. H. (2006) "Babies matter: pushing the gender equity revolution forward," in S. J. Bracken, J. K. Allen, and D. R. Dean (eds) *The Balancing Act: Gendered Perspectives in Faculty Roles and Work Lives*, Sterling, VA: Stylus.

Massoni, K. (2004) *The Influence of Gender on Students' Evaluation of Teachers, or, Why What we can't Count can Hurt us*, Kingston, RI: Sociologists for Women in Society.

Monks, J. (2009) "Who are the part-time faculty?," *Academe*, 95 (4): 33–37.

Preparing Future Faculty (2009) PFF Web, Washington, DC: Preparing Future Faculty. Online. Available http: http://www.preparing-faculty.org/ (accessed July 22, 2009).

Price, J., Cotton, S. R., Keeton, S., Burton, R., and Clifford Wittekind, J. E. (2002) *New Faculty Discuss the First Year as an Assistant Professor*, Washington, DC: American Sociological Association.

Risden, E. L. (1995) Book review. "The new faculty member: supporting and fostering professional development," *Journal of Higher Education*, 66 (1): 106–8.

Rosser, V. J. (2003) Review essay "Preparing and socializing new faculty members," *Review of Higher Education*, 26 (3): 387–95.

Silverman, F. H. (1999) *Publishing for Tenure and Beyond*, Westport, CT: Praeger.

Sorcinelli, M. D. (2007) "Faculty development: the challenge of going forward," *Peer Review*, 9 (4): 4–8.

Sprague, J., and Massoni, K. (2002) "How Students Evaluate Teachers: Gender Matters." Paper presented at the American Sociological Association, Chicago.

U.S. Department of Education, National Center for Education Statistics (2009) *Condition of Education. 2009*, Washington, DC: U.S. Department of Education.

Vesilind, P. A. (2000) *So You Want to Be a Professor? A Handbook for Graduate Students*, Thousand Oaks, CA: Sage.

West, M. S., and Curtis, J. W. (2006) *AAUP Faculty Gender Equity Indicators, 2006*, Washington, DC: American Association of University Professors.

Wieck, K. L. (2003) "Faculty for the millennium: changes needed to attract the emerging workforce into nursing," *Journal of Nursing Education*, 42: 151–58.

Wulff, D. H., and Austin, A. E. (2004) *Paths to the Professoriate: Strategies for Enriching the Preparation of Future Faculty*, San Francisco, CA: Jossey-Bass.

5 Teaching with intention

Technique, innovation and change in criminal justice education

Kristi Holsinger

One critical aspect, and some would argue the most important aspect, of an academic career is pedagogy, defined as the art, science, or profession of teaching. For me, teaching has become one of the most enjoyable parts of my job. The phrase "teaching with intention" implies that the teacher has certain goals in mind, has thoughtfully plotted a course of action, and that then, she or he implements that plan with determination and resolve. These teaching objectives don't remain stagnant as good teaching is the product of a dynamic, evolving process where every class and every semester provide an opportunity to rethink the effectiveness of various teaching approaches, and try new strategies. This evaluative process, with the benefit of student feedback, can facilitate an exciting and successful environment for learning in the classroom. Being willing to learn and grow in the role of teacher is essential and investing in teaching can make this component of your career satisfying and rewarding. Fortunately, we know quite a bit about what makes a great college professor.

Good teachers have the capacity to inspire their students in a way that allows their influence to be transformative and indelible. When criminal justice professors reflect on who *their* best professors were, they mention several key areas that made them outstanding teachers (Acker 2003). Not surprisingly, having passion and enthusiasm for the subject they teach and about teaching in general is critical and can be contagious. "Best professors" have been reported to have an abiding "compassion for humanity" and a commitment to "confront injustices." Similarly, another student wrote of his professor, "He expressed … a passion for learning, knowledge and something later I knew was justice" (Acker 2003: 223). Memorable teachers have an ability to make course material relevant by requiring critical thinking and analytical skills. Another quality identified in Acker's research on best teachers was setting high demands that require students to be prepared and rise to their highest potential. These teachers balanced high expectations with a high level of concern and commitment to each student's development. Good teachers were also remembered by their students in this research for their knowledge and expertise, organization, and capacity to communicate clearly (Acker 2003).

The ideals for good teaching are lofty, yet as an academic you'll be expected to balance this part of your career with research and service. The balance varies among institutions, and typically is given in terms of percentages indicating how your effort should be divided. It is important to gain knowledge about those expectations and determine whether this environment is a good fit for you, or to at the very least be aware of the requirements you will be evaluated by. Promotion and tenure are, in part, determined by how you meet these established standards. Therefore, this chapter begins with a discussion of how to advance professionally while maintaining a commitment to high-quality teaching.

To get the most satisfaction from teaching requires thoughtfulness on how to set up a good learning environment for you and your students, one that maintains student accountability and promotes student learning. To remain engaged and energized by teaching requires innovation. Innovation allows for expressions of creativity which for me has involved the development of some unique courses and approaches. One dimension of this examines the role of activism in the classroom and explores how to be an influential, even life-changing teacher in the lives of your students.

Advancing

Good teaching should be recognized, but often it is not, partly because of the difficulty in quantifying effectiveness. One way to acknowledge excellence in this realm is through the development of teaching awards within colleges and universities. Without this structure in place, departments typically rely on good teaching evaluations from students, which are often valid indicators of classroom performance, but also have their limitations. Faculty members are often concerned that student teaching evaluations reflect factors unrelated to teaching effectiveness, particularly the grade distribution of an instructor where higher grades correlate with higher teaching evaluations (Lersch and Greek 2001).

Where I work, teaching awards have been established at the departmental and college level to acknowledge and celebrate excellence in teaching. Faculty within most departments in our college nominate colleagues for this teaching award and a small committee, including the chair of the department, determine the recipient, who receives $500 and recognition. Each of these departmental awardees, as well as others nominated by peers, can submit an application packet for a college-level award which includes syllabi, letters of recommendation and support, numerical teaching evaluations as well as any other evidence of teaching effectiveness. In this way, there can be a broader representation of teaching effectiveness that goes beyond student evaluations. Several categories exist for different types of instructors, and a committee of previous awardees evaluate these packets. Winners receive $1,000 and have their picture placed on a wall in the dean's office that commemorates their accomplishment. In this way, institutions can send the message that good teaching matters and motivate faculty members to strive to improve their teaching.

I have no doubt that receiving the Distinguished Teaching Award in my department and the Dean's Outstanding Teaching Award for the College of

Arts and Science were influential in my own promotion. One contributing factor to my receiving these awards was that I had published articles about innovative teaching endeavors (discussed in depth later). Interestingly, it took my mentor's suggestion that I write up these experiences for me to even consider publishing them. In criminal justice, for example, there is a journal entitled *The Journal of Criminal Justice Education* which publishes articles addressing specific educational or academic issues. In this manner, a link is established between the highly valued practices of research and publishing and of teaching.

Including a well-developed teaching portfolio in promotion materials can be beneficial in achieving positive interim and tenure reviews, particularly from external reviewers. There are many materials in addition to course syllabi, standardized and qualitative summaries of student evaluations, and peer assessments of teaching that can be included in teaching portfolios. I included, for example, a statement on my teaching philosophy, a document illustrating the development of new teaching approaches within my classes and documentation of creative teaching endeavors. Remember that working with students on directed or independent projects, supervising or being on committees related to thesis, dissertation or comprehensive exam work are also important indicators of your commitment to teaching.

Learning

Class content often focuses on social problems that are related to students' personal experiences, and can even trigger crises for students. Feminist teachers must carefully consider how such issues can potentially impact students and affect their learning (Durfee and Rosenberg 2009). At the beginning of each semester, I prepare students by talking about what potentially difficult topics will be covered in class, and encourage students to think about whether they are ready to grapple with such issues. It is not always possible to anticipate one's emotional response, and therefore I also urge them to meet with me if they experience any difficulty with the course content. Prior to a class I prepare a list of community resources that may be helpful given the subjects covered. I have found that it is important to take the necessary time to listen attentively to students, respond with compassion, and provide appropriate referrals (see Durfee and Rosenberg 2009 for more on teaching sensitive issues).

There are a host of ways that student learning can be accomplished. Several examples are presented from a range of some of the approaches that I would recommend to facilitate a positive teaching and learning experience. It is critical, although not always easy, to create a respectful learning environment where different viewpoints and opinions are not only tolerated, but also encouraged and respected. One effective approach (borrowed from others) has been to start each class with a discussion of one of the policies in the syllabus. The policy states, "It is crucial to me that the classroom is a place where students demonstrate a sense of respect for others with differing life experiences.

I will do everything I can to encourage an environment where open and respectful dialogue can occur." As I say in class, when disagreements occur, the easiest response is to write that person off as an idiot. I encourage students to consider a more thoughtful, creative response, and to try and learn what life experiences have brought that person to the conclusions she or he is expressing. This reminder is given as needed (always more than once) through the course of the semester, particularly in regards to body language that communicates disregard.

Over the years I have developed a number of strategies to maintain student accountability and promote student learning. Course readings always result in a quiz, study questions to be completed, or the requirement that the content be clearly integrated into written papers. Not that all students do not read assigned materials, but it has been my experience that the majority do not unless held accountable in some meaningful grade-related way. Similarly, when ever possible I ask students to integrate readings with lectures, or lectures with out-of-class experiences.

Writing assignments are important for student learning. Consider making writing assignments as unique as possible to reduce the likelihood that students will purchase papers from the internet. Improving students' abilities to express themselves in writing is an important, but often neglected part of teaching. Regardless of whether you feel teaching writing is part of your job requirement, doing so, and devoting some class time to improving writing is in the best interest of your students (see Pfeifer and Ferree 2006 for ideas on how to teach writing skills).

Engaging lectures provide a wonderful opportunity to present realities and research that may not be common knowledge to the student population. There are countless advantages to this approach, and if done with some humor and spontaneity, lectures can create an environment of shared learning. This is particularly true if you maintain student engagement by eliciting their response to pertinent questions throughout the lecture. However, lectures also have significant limitations for student learning, most notably waning attention spans, and so developing other strategies that promote active learning and require greater student investment are worth incorporating to enhance your lectures (Robinson 2000).

Active learning strategies allow students to develop critical thinking and problem-solving skills, and can be empowering in helping them develop new competences. For example, the use of role playing, case studies, and debates that require developing valid arguements for the position they disagree with are all active learning approaches. These strategies allow greater imagination and creativity on the part of teachers as they can create learning experiences that permit students to answer big questions, take multiple perspectives, and feel empathy for persons different from themselves (Braswell and Whitehead 2002). In fact, one study found low empathy scores most strongly correlated with criminal justice majors, particularly with male students (Courtright et al. 2005). There are many approaches to draw on beyond the traditional lecture (some of which are noted below) and many of these, once established, will also reduce the time required in preparing a course based solely on lectures (see Myers and Myers 2008 and Robinson 2000 for criminal justice-related ideas for active learning in the classroom).

Students should be encouraged to do group work as they will be expected to "work well with others" in their careers and this task requires good communication skills. When doing group work in the classroom, I typically number students off to form groups of even size and to encourage students to interact with other students they may not know. For these experiences to run smoothly requires establishing very specific outcomes that are then reported back to the class. Checking in with groups and assisting them during the process aids in keeping students on track and engaged. In my Women, Crime and Criminal Justice class I use a case study of a fictional woman offender with multiple challenges. Each group of students takes a different perspective. One group plays the role of her family, another group her community, and finally a group who plays the role of the criminal justice professionals working with her. Discussion allows the class to explore how each group's needs assessment and recommendations overlap and conflict. This exercise allows students to engage in problem solving on their own and ensures a less sterile, more affective classroom experience (see Jones 2006 for benefits, examples, and ideas for assessing group work).

Recent trends in higher education include an emphasis on developing programs that provide outreach or service to the communities in which they are located. For example, the university I teach at has a mission statement and values that are consistent with this vision, expressed as having "both the opportunity and the obligation to serve this region and society by developing programs appropriate to its mission as an urban university." One method of fulfilling this mission is through service-learning opportunities for students. Service learning is an educational experience that allows students to address community needs (see Penn 2003 for a discussion of service learning). For many students, class material takes on new meaning when applied to real life situations. For example, volunteering with a local agency working to prevent sexual violence allows lessons to be learned that are largely inaccessible in the classroom. Students, for example, are able to more deeply understand obstacles to reporting sexual assaut and leaving violent living situations when they encounter survivors and their stories. Other ways of getting students relevant exposure to the community include having them interview professionals, conduct observations, and attend class-related community events.

Bringing guest speakers to class is an effective way to expose students to varying perspectives. In the field of criminal justice, those who have life experience, whether as offenders, victims, or criminal justice professionals, provide a real world application to textbooks and lectures. The guest speakers' impact will be even more significant if students prepare in advance by gaining some knowledge about the topic to be covered and develop thoughtful questions to ask. Critical analysis of material presented by the guest speakers in subsequent classes by way of reaction papers and class discussion only increase the learning opportunities for students (see Payne et al. 2003 for more ideas on using guest speakers in the classroom).

Films, particularly documentaries, are effective in exposing students to certain realities, and can challenge what students think they know. It is important either to avoid sensationalized media portrayals that do not reflect reality, or to show them as a method for providing contrast to reality. While viewing a movie in class, it is helpful to provide a handout of questions that relate the film to concepts covered in class, and to provide time for students to reflect on the content before the next class discussion. Some have used movies to teach ethics (Pino et al. 2009) and others have used works of fiction that provide a vehicle for teaching material covered in class with the benefit of developing critical thinking skills and empathy (see Engel 2003 for more ideas on teaching literature). The classes outlined below provide further illustrations of incorporating the strategies enumerated above.

Innovation: two examples

Class No. 1: College mentoring class with incarcerated girls

In collaboration with a professional from the local family court, I developed a mentoring class. (see Holsinger and Ayers 2004 for a more detailed presentation of this class). In this class, women college students act as mentors either to girls who are incarcerated or on probation. The motivation for this course came from research suggesting that system-involved girls could benefit from gender-specific programs that address girls' needs (Covington 1998; Greene Peters & Associates 1998). Specifically, Greene Peters & Associates (1998) recommend mentoring programs as among the promising approaches for girls. The class was designed to be responsive to the call for relational programming for system-involved girls and to allow the girls to benefit from one-on-one relationships with prosocial female role models. My own previous research found that most girls (in the local Family Court residential facility) wanted mentoring programs; however, this type of program was not available to them (Holsinger 2002).

Beyond the benefits to the girls, this experience serves a number of academic goals for college students as well. Students gain an in-depth first-hand knowledge of the life trajectory of system-involved girls, juvenile justice processing, and correctional interventions. Potential employment opportunities can be explored and the students can gain real world experience to supplement their program of study. This experience is particularly useful to criminal justice students as they prepare to enter professional occupations within the criminal and juvenile justice systems.

Beyond the expected completion of five contact hours with the girls per week, students are immersed in a learning experience that includes training sessions, required readings, and a comprehensive final paper about their experience. Initially, training involves the presentation of research about the unique circumstances and experiences of system-involved girls, the development of gender-specific programs, and information on how to most effectively work with and mentor this population. The court professional also conducts training to cover rules and procedures and gathers information required for background checks. In conjunction with the court professional, I provide supervision and support to the students while they are mentors. During the course, students are required to read materials that focus on the experiences and processing of system-involved girls and submit summary papers of relevant articles. A cumulative paper allows the students to reflect on knowledge gained about delinquent girls and their treatment, integrate course readings, and share personal insights gained from the course.

Using data collected from two semesters of teaching the mentoring class allowed an evaluation of the course. The mentored girls gave overwhelmingly positive feedback on the mentoring experience. It was also evident that this class had a profound impact on the college students, as demonstrated by themes that emerged in their final papers. Many of the mentors commented on their initial nervousness of meeting the girls, whom some referred to with phrases like "hard ghetto girls" and expressed concerns over what the girls would be like. The mentoring experience resulted in changed perceptions focusing on the strengths and the difficult life experiences of the girls, and generated empathy with the girls. The students also learned about how the juvenile justice system operates and gained insight into a career in juvenile justice. Another theme to emerge from the mentors' papers was their realization that the course was a mutually rewarding experience where they learned new skills and learned more about themselves too. Students noted that the experience gave them a new level of confidence to deal with new situations, made them less judgmental of others, and gave them a newfound sense of gratitude for things in their life they had previously taken for granted.

By the end of the class, the students were able to articulate a needs assessment leading to recommendations for juvenile correctional institutions that served girls. Mentors frequently noted that the girls just needed someone to listen to them, to love them, and to respond with empathy and acceptance. Many of the mentors identified "lack of guidance" as one of the main reasons the girls were in trouble in the first place. The mentors commented on the need for rules, structure, and boundaries from concerned adults in order for the girls to start making better choices. The mentors expressed that, by having good role models who offer encouragement, the girls would develop higher self-esteem and exhibit less delinquency. Many students noted the lack of programming and the frequency and duration of times when there was little for the girls to do, and suggested specific services that would help the girls with their problems; for example, one mentor wrote, "Implementing programs to help the girls deal with abuse is the very least that should be done." Another mentor suggested " ... programs dealing with relationships, life skills, study skills, parenting, job skills and drug prevention would be enormously helpful to the girls." The students' astute perceptions indicate that the issues are not overly complex and that there are clear and available solutions. Their papers demonstrated how the most pressing needs of the girls are unmet by the juvenile justice system and highlight many of the existing problems in the system. Notably, their insights show remarkable similarity to the work scholars are doing in this area in terms of the needs of system-involved girls.

Perhaps the most gratifying result of the course is the profound change in attitudes and beliefs by the students toward "delinquent" girls. Students recognize and articulate how the media shape their attitudes toward juvenile offenders and leads to punitive, fear-based responses. The students have the opportunity to see at first-hand that the conventional images of incarcerated girls in society do not match up to reality, and exposure to the girls is a critical component for public support of the development and implementation of more treatment-oriented services for girls in the legal system.

Class No. 2: Restorative justice class with incarcerated youth

I also developed a unique restorative justice class that I have been able to teach only one time (largely due to budget constraints in internally funded initiatives). The class consisted of traditional college students and incarcerated youth from a nearby residential facility. The course was an attempt to practice restorative justice principles by strengthening the damaged relationship between offenders and the community (see Holsinger and Crowther 2005 for a more detailed presentation of this class). Restorative justice, as an alternative to current criminal justice practices, provided interesting content for this course. Given the class make-up, we were able to examine this perspective from the viewpoint of college students and incarcerated youth. This approach seeks to meet the needs of all and repair the harm done by crime with an equal focus on the victim(s), the offender, and the community (Sullivan and Tifft 2001). The reintegration of offenders back into the community is another focal point of restorative justice (Braithwaite 1989). Common practices include victim–offender mediation, family group conferencing, and community service.

Previous research has found that exposure to juvenile offenders produces positive changes in college students' perceptions of offenders (Holsinger and Ayers 2004; Murray and Adams 1998; Vigorita 2002). This class also allows the students to become more aware of the broad range of issues faced by court-involved youth. An integral aspect of such awareness is an increase in tolerance for others and a greater awareness of issues surrounding diversity. Similarly, the college students gain deeper insights into the crime-related challenges faced by offenders, victims, communities, and justice agencies. This course again provides students with an opportunity to further explore careers in juvenile justice. For the high-school court-involved youth, I hoped that the class would provide them exposure to college life and help them envision college as an attainable goal. Consistent with the principles of restorative justice, this class allowed new relationships to develop that might increase the youth's sense of community, and hence facilitate their reintegration back into the community.

The college students and the court-involved youth met together one day a week (one additional class meeting was held each week with the college students). Class activities included a walking tour of campus, short lectures, and classroom group work which involved applying the principles of restorative justice to a variety of situations. This effort included exploring what it means to live out these ideals in our own interpersonal relationships and examining policies that cause societal harm. Discussions of obstacles to restorative justice included how to get past feelings of revenge, how to reintegrate victims and offenders when the community is dysfunctional, and how to overcome the challenges of delivering "needs-based justice" (Sullivan and Tifft 2001).

Using case studies of youth crime, students applied newly learned strategies of restorative justice to vignettes. One method used to generate discussions involved viewing the films *Dead Man Walking* and *Bowling for Columbine*. These movies allowed the students to examine nonrestorative aspects of our society. A family court professional came in as a guest speaker, and shared real life examples of her work using restorative justice principles in the local juvenile court. The youth also took the college students on a tour of the correctional facility where they were housed. They were able to explain various programs they participated in and detail the basic structure of life in this particular correctional facility. Another speaker invited to talk to the class was a man recently released from a Death Row sentence on a wrongful conviction. He came to the class and shared his story. Again, this speaker provided a forum for discussion on the use of restorative justice principles to repair the damage done to exonerated prisoners.

Community service is one restorative justice method that can be used in the criminal justice system that requires offenders to repair harm done to communities. In this vein, the entire restorative justice class volunteered at a local community food network that partners with over 500 charitable agencies to provide food to local hunger relief agencies. This activity gave the class exposure to volunteering and the opportunity to do something to give back to the community. Although it would have been ideal to find a project that involved victims of crime, the community service project was a time of fun and bonding for the group. The experience demonstrated to the students (many for the first time) the rewarding nature of volunteer work that benefits the community.

The one class each week where just the college students met provided time for additional readings and assignments. An in-class project for this group of students required the design and implementation of a survey to measure public opinions toward youth crime as well as beliefs about solutions. The class also toured the local detention facility where all of the court-involved students had been prior to their current placement. This activity was designed to provide a better understanding of how the juvenile justice system operates. At the end of the class, there was a luncheon ceremony at a nearby restaurant where framed certificates were given to the court-involved students and the class experience was celebrated.

The college students positively evaluated the course, largely because it was a different style of class compared to the more traditional classes they had taken. Memorable moments for the college students included the speaker who was an exonerated Death Row inmate, the field trips to the facility where the youth lived and to the detention center, and finally the community service project. The interaction between the students and youth was a valuable and enjoyable experience reported by the majority of the college students. In the final assignment, half of the college students referred to the interaction with the incarcerated youth as the most enjoyable part of the class. This interaction gave the college students an opportunity to learn about the lives of the court-involved youth.

Like the mentoring class, one of the most noticeable themes reflected by all of the college students was the change in attitudes toward "juvenile delinquents." The college students wrote that they learned they had more in common with the youth than they previously thought, and that the youth were capable of change and achieving success in their lives. For some, it provided them with direction regarding their future careers. The consensus among the college students was that this course had a positive impact on the younger court-involved students. Virtually all of the students believed that the youth learned they could succeed in a college-level course. Most of the students observed that the youth learned that there are people out there who want to help and are interested in them and what they have to say.

A majority of the college students noted that our current system is overly punitive in its response to juvenile crime. The trip by the college students to the detention facility was a particularly eye-opening experience. Several students noted that the facilities and living environment of the youth under court supervision were not entirely suitable to a rehabilitative approach. As a result of learning about an alternative solution to the nation's juvenile crime problem, and by studying and seeing at first-hand certain aspects of our current system, the students had many specific ideas on changes needed in the juvenile justice system. One improvement mentioned by many students was the need for caring and passionate staff to work with the youth. All of the students believed restorative justice principles and programming provide a good alternative to the punitive system now in place and offer victims greater involvement in the justice process. Positive media coverage provided an upbeat ending to the restorative justice class. An article ran in the local paper titled, "Students Seek New Solutions to Crime." The story served to educate the public of the potential of the youth currently involved in the juvenile justice system and presented new, nonpunitive ways of responding to juvenile crime.

Changing

As a graduate student, something I read by Meda Chesney-Lind truly resonated with me, but also contrasted with certain aspects of graduate school training. She wrote that a feminist perspective includes activism where research informs policy and improves the lives of incarcerated females, or other marginalized groups (Chesney-Lind 1991). It made sense to me that social science research could be a vehicle for social justice; a way to inform policy and change institutions without being an automatic compromise of objectivity by the social scientist. My initial focus (with the mentorship of Joanne Belknap) was on girls caught up in various parts of the juvenile justice system.

Eventually, I began to broaden my definition of activism to include the impact my classes could have on students. Can students' subjective perceptions change with critical pedagogy? Can the acquisition of knowledge form the ground work for liberating social change? How do I inspire and empower students to be social justice advocates who thoughtfully engage in the issues facing their communities? Braswell and Whitehead (2002) note that teachers often focus on conveying the present reality of how things are without focusing enough time on how things could be different, or how things should be. "We are not just teaching our students about criminal justice and criminology, we are also teaching them about the larger landscape of life – about their potential for making a difference in the world around them" (p. 348).

Inspired by the mentoring and restorative justice classes, and the changes I saw in my students, I began to incorporate more of an activist orientation into my more traditional criminal justice classes. In Missouri (a few miles from the Kansas border), like in many parts of the country, it is not uncommon to encounter students with punitive, fear-based attitudes toward crime. My personal experience has been that the student body seems more likely to defend the status quo than challenge it. Work and family commitments also consume students' time in ways that do not leave much time or energy for activism.

One way I attempt to gauge the change that takes place in students is to give a pretest to measure class attitudes and beliefs related to the content of the class. At the end of the class, a posttest is used to examine attitudinal changes by the students. In addition to basic demographics such as age, race, sex, academic major, and several open-ended questions, I typically ask questions that tap into issues such as their beliefs about whether the current correctional system is too harsh, too lenient, or just right.

In one correction class, 30 percent of the students initially thought the current correctional system was too harsh, and by the end of the class 78 percent of the class felt that way. When asked if prisoners are coddled by receiving too many privileges, less than half of the class disagreed (45 percent), but posttest results showed that the vast majority (87 percent) disagreed. Most students (92 percent) felt that rehabilitation should be one of the goals of the correctional system; however, that number increased to 100 percent by the end of the class. Another question addressed whether students perceived incarceration to be practiced in a racist way. In a class that was 31 percent African-American, the percentage of students agreeing with this statement increased from 32 percent to 63 percent over the course of the class. Most students did not originally see punishment as the most effective way of improving a person's behavior (63 percent); however, by the end of the class, the percentatge of students who felt that way went up to 91 percent. Why did these changes occur? It is difficult to know for sure, but student feedback indicated that making classes memorable by doing interactive, engaging, and unusual classroom activities in addition to lectures played a role.

Another way to address change materialized when I was asked to teach a Capstone course (senior seminar class for criminal justice majors). Since few criminal justice classes attempt to get at the root of our individual concepts of justice, I structured the class around the theme of "pursuing justice." In this class we explore where our ideas of justice come from, what strategies exist to address injustice as well as more difficult questions like "What are our moral and ethical responsibilities when we are exposed to injustice?" and "How relevant is the criminal justice perspective in addressing social injustice?" The class objectives include exploring how the students' knowledge base can contribute to their future roles as citizens, employees and activists, and to explore their personal career goals. In order to achieve these objectives, a significant portion of the class works to improve students' critical thinking skills in conjunction with their public speaking and writing skills. For example, one assignment involves selecting a documentary movie that deals with a justice issue. The students orally summarize the movie for the class, and discuss how the content is related to justice, and outline strategies that could be used to achieve justice.

At the close of the class, I remind the students that they are now experts in correction in a way that the general public is not. They possess much more factual information that makes them capable of speaking about criminal justice-related issues, and I encourage them to do exactly that. Writing editorials in response to criminal justice-related stories that appear in the news media is their right and obligation (and one I have them practice in the classroom). Clearly, change in students' subjective perceptions can happen in the classroom. The more difficult question to answer is whether the acquisition of this knowledge will lay the ground work for social change and whether students have been inspired and empowered to be social justice advocates within their communities. It is my hope, as their teacher, that it has.

Conclusion

As you embark on a career that involves teaching I urge you to teach with intention. It is worth the time to think about what you hope your students will learn from you and what kind of a professor you aspire to become. Be creative in thinking about how teaching can be part of your own advancement in your career and take full advantage of the freedom to try new and innovative approaches in teaching. You may come to find that it is the most enjoyable and rewarding part of your profession.

References

Acker, J. (2003) "Class acts: Outstanding college teachers and the difference they make," *Criminal Justice Review*, 28 (2): 215–31.

Braithwaite, J. (1989) *Crime, Shame and Reintegration*, New York: Cambridge University Press.

Braswell, M., and Whitehead, J. T. (2002) "'In the beginning was the student': Teaching peacemaking and justice issues," *Crime and Delinquency*, 48 (2): 333–49.

Chesney-Lind, M. (1991) "Patriarchy, prisons and jails: A critical look at trends in women's incarceration," *Prison Journal*, 71: 51–67.

Courtright, K. E., Mackey, D. A., and Packard, S. H. (2005) "Empathy among college students and criminal justice majors: Identifying predispositional traits and the role of education," *Journal of Criminal Justice Education*, 16 (1): 125–44.

Covington, S. (1998) "The relational theory of women's psychological development: Implications for the criminal justice system," in R. T. Zaplin (ed.) *Female Offenders: Critical Perspectives and Effective Interventions*, Gaithersburg, MD: Aspen, 113–31.

Durfee, A., and Rosenberg, K. (2009) "Teaching sensitive issues: Feminist pedagogy and the practice of advocacy-based counselling," *Feminist Teacher*, 19 (2):103–21.

Engel, S. T. (2003) "Teaching literature in the criminal justice curriculum," *Journal of Criminal Justice Education*, 14 (2): 345–54.

Greene Peters & Associates (1998) *Guiding Principles for Promising Female Programming: An Inventory of Best Practices*, Washington DC: Office of Juvenile Justice and Delinquency Prevention.

Holsinger, K. (2002) *An Evaluation of Needs and Services of System-involved Youth: Developing Gender-specific Services for Jackson County Girls*. Final report for the Jackson County Family Court, Kansas City: University of Missouri.

Holsinger, K., and Ayers, P. (2004) "Mentoring in juvenile facilities: Connecting college students with incarcerated girls," *Journal of Criminal Justice Education*, 15 (2): 351–72.

Holsinger, K., and Crowther, A. (2005) "College course participation for incarcerated youth: Bringing restorative justice to life," *Journal of Criminal Justice Education*, 16 (2): 328–39.

Jones, P. R. (2006) "Using groups in criminal justice courses: Some new twists on a traditional pedagogical tool," *Journal of Criminal Justice Education*, 17 (1): 87–102.

Lersch, K. M., and Greek, C. (2001) "Exploring the beliefs surrounding student evaluations of instruction in criminology and criminal justice undergraduate courses," *Journal of Criminal Justice Education*, 12 (2): 283–99.

Murray, J. L., and Adams, D. C. (1998) "Developmental implications of undergraduate student attitudes concerning juvenile justice," *NASPA Journal*, 35: 245–54.

Myers, L. B., and Myers, L. J. (2008) *Classroom Activities for Criminal Justice*, Belmont, CA: Thomson Wadsworth.

Payne, B. K., Sumter, M., and Sun, I. (2003) "Bringing the field into the criminal justice classroom: Field trips, ride-alongs, and guest speakers," *Journal of Criminal Justice Education*, 14 (2): 327–44.

Penn, E. B. (2003) "Service-learning: A tool to enhance criminal justice," *Journal of Criminal Justice Education*, 14 (2): 371–83.

Pfeifer, H. L., and Ferree, C. W. (2006) "Tired of 'reeding' bad papers? Teaching research and writing skills to criminal justice students," *Journal of Criminal Justice Education*, 17 (1): 121–42.

Pino, N. W., Brunson, R. K., and Stewart, E. A. (2009) "Using movies to illustrate ethical dilemmas in undergraduate criminal justice courses," *Journal of Criminal Justice Education*, 20 (2): 194–202.

Robinson, M. B. (2000) "Using active learning in criminal justice: Twenty-five examples," *Journal of Criminal Justice Education*, 11 (1): 65–78.

Sullivan, D., and Tifft, L. (2001) *Restorative Justice: Healing the Foundations of our Everyday Lives*, Monsey, NY: Willow Tree Press.

Vigorita, M. S. (2002) "Planning and implementing a criminal justice course with university students and youthful offenders," *Journal of Criminal Justice Education*, 13 (2): 404–32.

6 A brief guide to academic publishing

Claire M. Renzetti

How would you like to see your name in lights? Okay, maybe not in lights, but boldly staring back at you on the printed page? Seeing one's name for the first time on a published journal article or book cover is a thrill few forget. In fact, although some of my colleagues probably will not admit it, no matter how much one publishes, it is always satisfying to see one's name and one's work on the printed page. But we publish our work not only for personal gratification – to stoke our egos, if you will; we also publish to contribute to the knowledge base of our disciplines, to inform policy makers and practitioners about significant findings that should be considered in legislation and program development, and to help remedy specific social problems. In other words, we publish to make a difference in the world. And, of course, we publish because we have to; the quantity and quality of one's publications weigh heavily in tenure and promotion decisions at most colleges and universities. If we want to keep our jobs – and, increasingly, if we want to even get a job – as well as advance our careers, we must publish. The old dictum "Publish or perish" haunts many new academics who are also busy preparing and teaching courses, advising students, and serving on departmental and university committees. The primary goal of this chapter is to take some of the stress out of academic publishing by offering advice on the processes of both journal and book publishing.

When conducting workshops on publishing, one thing that consistently stands out among those who attend is how daunting, even frightening, the publishing process appears. In some ways, this is because they are new to the process and anything one hasn't tried before can be intimidating. Serious concerns about getting published, however, also stem largely from the fact that so much is riding on this; new academics come to the publishing workshops because they know their jobs, their future in their careers, depend on getting published.

More specifically, then, my goals in this chapter are to remove the mystery surrounding publishing and reduce the anxiety that often accompanies the process. I will offer step-by-step advice on dealing with various aspects of publishing, first with regard to peer-reviewed journals, and second with regard to books. Although I certainly cannot guarantee that my advice will get you published, I can say that it derives from years of experience of being on both sides of the publishing process as an editor and as an author. Since the early 1990s, I have been the editor of two book series as well as the editor of the peer-reviewed journal *Violence Against Women* (*VAW*). *VAW* is published monthly, and we receive more than 300 manuscript submissions each year. Needless to say, I spend a good bit of my time reading book and journal manuscripts and reading reviews of books and journal manuscripts. But I also submit my own work for peer review; I have authored or edited sixteen books and many book chapters and journal articles since receiving my PhD in 1981. Does all of this make me an expert on academic publishing? Hardly, and some of my equally or more experienced colleagues may disagree with one piece of advice or another that I proffer here. Nevertheless, I am a firm believer in learning from experience, my own and others, and I pass along this advice in that spirit.

The journal article

Let's begin with the assumption that you have conducted a well-designed research project that addresses important questions. As Robinson (1988) points out, many pieces on publishing "how to's" never get far beyond discussions of explaining what a good study should look like. However, the fact is that coming up with a good idea and translating it into a sound research project should be a given by the time one gets to the publishing stage. "What we want to know now is how to increase our chances of getting competent work published" (Robinson 1988: 153).

My first piece of advice is do your homework on the journals. What I mean by this is do not submit your manuscript to a journal just because the journal title sounds like one that publishes work on your topic, or because your mentor or a colleague or friend has published work on your topic in a certain journal, or even because an article you like and cite in your manuscript has been published in that journal or simply because the journal is prestigious. Your research may be excellent and your manuscript well written, but if it is not compatible with the mission and focus of a specific journal, it will not be accepted for publication. Therefore, engage in strategic publishing.[1] Go on line or to the library and read a few issues of several journals that you think might be a good fit for your manuscript. Ask yourself not only whether a specific journal publishes work on your topic, but also whether that journal publishes work that uses your methodology and analysis strategy. Some journals, for example, do not publish much, if any, qualitative research, so even if a journal publishes articles on your topic, if all or the majority of those articles use rather sophisticated statistical tests to analyze data and your data are derived from in-depth interviews, you may wish to reconsider submitting your manuscript to that journal. If your research has interdisciplinary implications, you may consider looking at journals that fall outside the confines of your discipline or, more narrowly, outside the subfield of your discipline, but that publish work from multiple related disciplines or subfields.

Given that many journals charge nonrefundable submission fees, identifying journals that are a good fit for your manuscript is also a cost-saving measure. Besides investigating the mission of a journal and the types of articles published in it, it is also helpful to find out its acceptance rate. Some professional associations offer guides to journals that include information such as length of time from submission to a publication and the Impact Factor and ranking in *Journal Citation Reports*, as well as acceptance rates (see, for example, American Sociological Association 2009). While every author wants to publish in the most "prestigious" journal possible, it is also important to be realistic. That is not to say you should not submit your work to journals with very low acceptance rates. Rather, you should keep in mind that in such cases the probability of your manuscript being accepted for publication may be small, although to be honest, knowing this may do little to ease the disappointment when a rejection letter arrives.

Another way to test for goodness of fit for your manuscript is to query the editor. I receive several email messages a week from authors asking if their work might be of interest to the readers of *VAW* or if their topic falls within the parameters of the journal's mission. I welcome such inquiries, and I think most journal editors do, but I will offer a caution: Your query should not be a general fishing expedition. I get many messages that simply say the sender has written a manuscript on a particular topic, the abstract is included, and she or he wants to know if I am interested in publishing it. If the topic of the manuscript addresses any aspect of *VAW*'s rather broad mission, I encourage the sender to submit the manuscript, adding the disclaimer that this in no way assures publication, since the manuscript must undergo peer review. If the author had looked at recent issues of the journal, though, she or he would know this. More productive, I think, are queries that ask specific questions. Examples of such queries are: "My manuscript exceeds the page limit posted for submissions because it includes lengthy excerpted quotes from interviews. May I still submit it?" and "I noticed in perusing recent journal issues that none of the articles use a case study method. Do you publish articles that report the results of case studies?" Such queries indicate to me that the author has already done some preliminary investigation of the journal and has a genuine interest in publishing her or his work there; the author just wants to be certain that the manuscript meets the journal's style requirements or is appropriate in terms of methodological focus.[2]

This discussion leads to a related point: When investigating a journal's content, also take the time to familiarize yourself with the journal's style in terms of article structure as well as citation and referencing format. For instance, some journals require that the abstract be prepared according to a specific format in which subheadings are used (research question, sample, methods, findings, conclusions), whereas others require a one-paragraph summary that may include all of these elements but in a narrative style. Similarly, the referencing style of a law review article is very different from that of a typical criminology or sociology journal. Small differences (e.g., ASA versus APA citation and reference style) likely will not matter to editors or reviewers, at least at the submission stage, but when a manuscript has been prepared in a style dramatically different from that used by the journal to which it was submitted it may suggest to the editor and reviewers that: (1) the author did not take the time to familiarize herself or himself with the journal, raising the question of the author's genuine interest in placing her or his work in that journal; or (2) the author submitted the manuscript to a journal with different style requirements, it was subsequently rejected, and the author was too lazy or disinterested to revise the manuscript to conform to the present journal's style requirements before submitting it there. Neither may be true, but why let something that is so easy to correct give an editor or reviewer a negative impression of you as an author?

Another common source of negative impressions is a poorly prepared manuscript. I raise the issue here because it is something that should be corrected before the manuscript is submitted. Proofread[3] your manuscript carefully before submission. Manuscripts plagued by typos and grammatical errors distract reviewers from the important matter at hand – the manuscript's substantive content. If you are not a careful proofreader, enlist the assistance of a friend or colleague who is. Even if you are a careful proofreader, a second set of eyes looking for typos rather than reading for content is helpful.

Once you are ready to submit your manuscript, follow the submission instructions carefully. Peer-reviewed journals require "blind" submission, meaning that the manuscript should contain no author-identifying information. While most authors understand this to mean that the title page should not contain their name and institutional affiliation, many nevertheless include an acknowledgment note that may make author identification fairly easy for reviewers. Refrain from including acknowledgments until the manuscript has been accepted for publication. Similarly, many authors cite their own work, which is not problematic in itself unless it leads to author identification in its specificity (e.g., "The present paper takes up a question that I was unable to address in an earlier study" and then the citation gives the author's name and publication date and the full reference is listed in the references section). One way to avoid author identification in such instances is to substitute for the parenthetical citation the phrase, "authorship withheld to ensure blind review," and to exclude the reference until after the manuscript has been accepted for publication. Although fully blind review is sometimes impossible, it is important to keep in mind that one reason it was adopted was to protect authors; we wish our work to be evaluated on its merits, not on the basis of name recognition, or worse yet, on the basis of whether a reviewer likes us or is holding a grudge against us.

Submission of a manuscript to a peer-reviewed journal carries with it the author's assurance that the work has not been previously published nor is it under simultaneous review at another journal. Simultaneous submission of the same manuscript to multiple journals is unethical, which is why many journals explicitly request that authors make such an assurance upon submission.

Because many journals now use online submission systems, submission has become easier. Moreover, new academics under pressure from the ticking tenure clock may be tempted to submit a manuscript to more than one journal simultaneously, given that the review process may take several months at each journal and time is a luxury they do not have. Do not succumb to this temptation. If simultaneous submission is discovered – and it is more easily discoverable than you might think – editors will typically pull the manuscript from consideration and notify the author of the reason. While this ethical breach may not follow you for the rest of your career – after all, everyone makes mistakes – you will be no further ahead in terms of getting your work into print; indeed, you may be further behind.

Dealing with reviews and publication decisions

Authors and editors, as the previous paragraph implies, have a trust relationship. Editors trust that authors are submitting original work that has not already been published elsewhere and is not under simultaneous review at another journal. Authors, on the other hand, entrust to editors the task of insuring that their manuscript will receive timely, fair, and constructive evaluation. The wait for reviewer feedback and a publication decision is an anxious period for authors, especially those early in their careers, and the longer the wait, the more anxious they become. I know the words probably sound hollow to anyone who has waited six months or longer for reviews and a decision letter, but editors do understand the anxiety-producing nature of the process, and we do our best to make it as efficient and expeditious as possible. Nevertheless, delays may occur for several reasons. One reason is difficulty in enlisting reviewers for a manuscript. For *VAW*, we require two independent peer reviews per manuscript; some journals require three, four, or more. Given that *VAW* receives more than 300 submissions per year, sheer volume requires a very large reviewer pool. Not infrequently – in fact, far more frequently than I would like – at least one of the individuals initially invited to review a manuscript declines. Some who decline suggest alternative reviewers, but many do not. Consequently, editors must identify additional individuals who are knowledgeable about the topic and methods of the research presented in the manuscript. Although it may not appear to be the case sometimes, every editor I know takes seriously the task of matching competent reviewers with specific manuscripts. Depending on how many invitations must be sent before an editor receives the requisite number of reviewers, it may be several weeks following submission before a manuscript is actually under review. The adage "Do unto others ... " is worth mentioning here. When invited to review a manuscript that has been submitted to a journal give serious consideration not only to whether you have the time to complete the review by the deadline, but also whether the topic and methodology are within your areas of expertise.

Editors typically give reviewers three or four weeks to provide their evaluation and make a recommendation regarding publication. Most journals have a form for reviewers to complete with fixed response categories indicating their assessment of factors such as the significance of the research for the field, the appropriateness of the manuscript for the journal, the quality of the research, and the quality of the writing. Reviewers are also encouraged to write a narrative evaluation, highlighting the specific strengths and weaknesses of the manuscript with particular attention to how the latter may be rectified. These narrative evaluations are of course shared with authors, but reviewers may also offer comments for the editor only, and usually the reviewers' actual recommendation regarding publication is not shared with the author.

This process gives rise to two other possible sources of delay in returning reviews and a decision letter to authors. First, reviewers are often late in submitting their reviews, despite repeated reminders and even personal contacts from the editor. Second, editors may decide to return a review to a reviewer for revision if the editor feels that the assessment is too personal in a negative way or offers nothing in terms of constructive feedback. Fortunately, my sense is that this latter scenario rarely occurs, but when it does occur, the review process is further delayed.

Here, too, the adage "Do unto others … " applies. If you have agreed to review a manuscript, adhere to the deadline. A brief delay is understandable and excusable, but submitting a review several weeks beyond the deadline – or not submitting it at all once you have agreed to review – is unfair to the author and the editor and very unprofessional. Moreover, take care in your review to use a collegial tone and avoid sarcasm. Provide constructive comments. This does not mean that you should overlook or downplay flaws in the manuscript or the research. Rather, be specific when identifying a problem or weakness and offer the author suggestions for rectifying it, if possible.

There are essentially three publication outcomes from the peer review process: the manuscript is rejected and will be given no further consideration; the author is asked to revise in light of the reviewers' feedback and resubmit the manuscript for further consideration; or the manuscript is accepted as it is or with only minor revisions. I will address each outcome in turn.

Rejection. No one likes being rejected, either socially or professionally. Yet, there is not a single academic colleague whom I know who has not received a rejection letter from a journal editor. When I have to deliver this news to authors, I always write that I realize they do not enjoy receiving such a letter, nor do I enjoy having to send it. And I mean that sincerely, since I know, too well perhaps, the disappointment of having one's work rejected for publication. But in conversations with authors I have come to understand that reading the rejection letter is often far less painful than having to digest the reviewers' feedback. Despite explicit instructions to provide constructive feedback and not to personalize critiques, reviewers' evaluations are sometimes biting at best and hurtful at worst. In some cases, reviewers' comments may strike the author as incomprehensible, as if the reviewer must have read a different manuscript altogether. One's first reactions to a rejection letter and negative reviews may be anger and frustration, which is why it is often a good idea to put the reviews aside for a few days after the initial read and return to glean constructive feedback in a calmer frame of mind.

When reading reviews identify the specific reasons the manuscript was rejected. If the primary reason is that it was not suitable for the journal to which you submitted it, then you need to discern why and look for a more appropriate publication outlet for your work. Helpful reviewers often suggest alternative journals that they think may be a better fit for the manuscript. But typically when a manuscript is rejected it is because reviewers feel there are serious flaws in the study design or analysis. A detailed discussion of all the various reasons that reviewers may give for recommending against publication of a given manuscript is beyond the scope of this chapter. Suffice it to say, however, that unless a review is an obviously blatant personal attack on the author, you should take the reviews seriously and read them scrupulously; unpleasant as that may be, the reviews are intended to help you improve your manuscript, which may ultimately increase your chances of getting it published elsewhere. It may also be beneficial to ask a more experienced colleague familiar with the manuscript to read the reviews and help you digest them, particularly if you find some comments confusing or you are unsure how to interpret specific criticisms or suggestions.

Revise. Much of this advice also pertains to the revise and resubmit (R&R) decision, except that since the manuscript will likely – though not always – be sent back to the same reviewers once it is resubmitted, carefully addressing each reviewer's concerns is imperative. If reviewers identify significant gaps in your literature review, fill those gaps. If the reviewers ask for clarification of a point, clarify it. If they want your rationale for using a specific method or statistical test, explain it. If they want further discussion of certain points, elaborate. Although some authors (e.g., Frey 2003) have made the claim that the peer-review process is similar in some ways to prostitution, since it may force authors to compromise their ideas in order to get published and thereby attain academic "success," I disagree.[4] In my experience, including my experience as an author, I have found that peer reviews nearly always strengthen a manuscript. If a reader cannot understand what a writer is trying to say, the value – that is, the potential impact – of the work may be lost, and no researcher should allow that to happen simply because they are too stubborn or proud to alter their writing as requested by a reviewer.

That said, it is sometimes the case that an author feels strongly that a reviewer is simply incorrect or that making a requested revision will alter the intended meaning or weaken rather than strengthen a manuscript. My advice to authors in such situations is that it is their work and they should not change something solely to appease a reviewer. When resubmitting a revised manuscript, authors are usually asked to track and explain the changes they made. I advise authors to also explain why they chose not to make specific revisions. In most cases, a sound rationale will be understood by editors and reviewers.

A common mistake that authors – especially new authors – make is assuming that a revised manuscript will be recommended for publication by reviewers subsequent to their reassessment of it. Sometimes reviewers recommend further revision necessitating another review cycle, and sometimes, even though the author thinks he or she adequately addressed the reviewers' criticisms, the reviewers recommend against publication. Nevertheless, editors do not typically give R&R decisions unless a manuscript has a good probability of being accepted once the author has tended to the reviewers' concerns and suggestions.

Accepted. So, let us assume that your manuscript has been accepted for publication. In addition to the acceptance letter, you will likely receive a set of instructions detailing how the manuscript should be prepared for production. Read these instructions and *follow them* carefully. It is your responsibility to ensure, for instance, that the citation and referencing format in your manuscript conforms exactly to that used by the journal, that the references are complete, that permissions have been obtained if they are necessary, and so on. Do not expect the editor or the editorial assistant or the publisher to do this work for you. Failure to follow the manuscript preparation instructions could result in the manuscript being returned to you – perhaps more than once – for corrections and that simply delays getting it into print.

The "production of scholarship" in the form of articles published in peer-reviewed professional journals is, as Karen Staller (2007: 138) has noted, the result of "extensive conversations among authors, editors, and referees." But as Staller also points out, the scholarly production process is rarely "operationalized" for new faculty apart from the imperatives to publish "a lot" and to publish in "top-tier" journals. Hopefully, the discussion thus far has provided enough concrete information to demystify the process somewhat and make it less intimidating, especially for those new to academe. Let us turn now to the process of book publishing.

The book

The process of publishing a book differs in several significant ways from the process of publishing a journal article. For one thing, authors frequently do not submit completed book manuscripts to publishers; they submit instead a book proposal along with perhaps one or two draft chapters. This material is reviewed by the editor and in many cases by several peer reviewers. The editor may subsequently ask the author to respond to reviewers' concerns and/or revise the proposal and resubmit it. And at some publishing houses, assuming favorable assessments by the editor and reviewers, the proposal, sample chapters and reviews must be presented to an editorial board for approval before a contract is offered.

For much of the remainder of this chapter I will focus on the book proposal, but first I wish to briefly address one question that, as a series editor, I am often asked by recent PhDs: Should I send a publisher my dissertation? My consistent answer is: No, send a proposal for a book based on your dissertation research, then work hard on rewriting your dissertation into a book. This is probably a discouraging reply to many given the time and effort that goes into researching and writing the dissertation. This research and writing may result in an out-standing piece of scholarship that is well written and may even break new ground. But keep in mind that the dissertation is written to win the approval of a very specific audience – the dissertation committee – and to fulfill the requirements of an academic degree. As such, it likely conforms to a style and contains a large amount of material that, to put it politely, may not be as sti-mulating or impressive to a wider audience, even an audience composed of other scholars in one's field. As William Germano (2005) points out, the for-mula for a dissertation – including demonstrating with countless citations and footnotes that one has read all that has been written on the topic at hand – is not the recipe for producing a good book. I strongly recommend that new PhDs who wish to publish their dissertation research in book form consult Germa-no's excellent guide *From Dissertation to Book* for invaluable down-to-earth advice on how to successfully revise the dissertation into a publishable book manuscript.

The book proposal[5]

Again, we will begin with the assumption that you have conducted a well-designed study about which you would like to write a book, or that you have a compelling idea for a book. The first step toward getting the book published is to convince a publisher that this is a worthwhile project. After all, the publisher will be investing substantial resources in seeing the project through to completion and marketing it to its intended audiences. The proposal is your opportunity to make the case for why your book should be published.

Begin by introducing the topic of your book and explain why you are writing it. Why is this an important topic to write about? What specific issues will you cover in the book? What goals do you expect to achieve by writing this book? You also need to distinguish your book from other books about your topic already on the market. You should identify each major competing title along with the author, publisher and year of publication, and explain how your book is different – and, hopefully, better – than the books already published on your topic. Do you take a new approach to the topic, apply or develop a particular theoretical perspective, or use data that have not been analyzed previously? Tell the publisher what is unique about your book.

Publishers are also interested in your target audience. For whom are you writing the book? A common mistake authors make is to claim that the book will appeal to *all* audiences – professionals, students, policy makers, practi-tioners, the general public. While an author wishes her or his book to be read by the largest, broadest audience possible, no book can be all things to all people. You need to be clear regarding your primary audience. If your book is likely to be of interest to other audiences, by all means identify them and explain why the book will likely appeal to them. Publishers also want to gauge a book's potential for classroom use. It is helpful for the author to identify specific courses in which the book might be adopted as a primary or supplemental text rather than simply list general subjects (e.g., "the book may be used as a supplemental text in a course on Gender, Race, Class and Crime" as opposed to simply "the book may be used in Criminology courses"). It is also helpful to identify the level of these courses (e.g., undergraduate, advanced undergraduate, graduate).

Another important element of the proposal is the schedule. Provide an estimated date of when you expect a first and/or a final draft to be completed. Depending on the publishing schedule – e.g., some publishers release books seasonally, such as fall and spring, while others bring books out every month – a publisher will want some sense of when the author expects to complete the project; this affects the publisher's budget, marketing plans, and the like. Be realistic. I have a set of Post-it notes on my desk that read, "I love deadlines. I love the whooshing sound they make as they fly by." Deadlines tend to arrive much faster than one anticipates when setting them. I advise authors to build extra time into their anticipated completion dates. That way, if something unexpected occurs in their personal or professional lives, they will have a cushion of time for completing the project without disrupting the production schedule. And if the book is finished ahead of schedule, so much the better.[6]

Scheduling may be somewhat more difficult when you are editing a book, rather than authoring it. In the case of an edited volume of original chapters, you are dependent on your contributors to meet the deadlines you impose – and as anyone who has edited a book will likely tell you, it is rare for all contributors to send their chapters on time. Typically, editors request first drafts of chapters from contributors and must build in time not only for contributors to write the chapters, but also for those chapters to be reviewed by the editor(s) and perhaps others and feedback offered. Then contributors must be given time to revise their chapters and editors need time to review final drafts, compile the chapters and put finishing touches to the manuscript (e.g., write the preface and/or introduction, section introductions, a conclusion) before sending it to the publisher. Working out the schedule, then, can be a bit like fortune telling and it is of course impossible to plan for every contingency or potential disruption, but by being generous to yourself with the schedule you can reduce stress and pose minimal threat to the production schedule when, for example, a contributor of a critical chapter backs out and a new author for that chapter must be enlisted, or a chapter or two require multiple drafts before they are ready for publication.[7]

A publisher also needs to assess an author's qualifications for writing the proposed book. You should include a copy of your vita with the proposal, but in the proposal itself provide a brief biographical statement that informs the publisher of your expertise in the area about which you are writing. If your book will be an edited collection of original chapters, it is best to have as many, if not all, of the contributors identified – and hopefully, already in agreement to write their respective chapters – as possible. Include in the proposal a brief bio statement for each contributor that establishes her or his expertise in the subject about which she or he will be writing.

The final component of the proposal is the outline of the book's contents. This is more than simply a table of contents with chapter titles. For each chapter include a summary of what the chapter will cover. Keep in mind that, like the title you have given the book, at this stage the chapter coverage is somewhat tentative. The actual content of the book is likely to evolve and change as you write as well as in response to feedback from the publishing editor and reviewers. The purpose of the outline is to give the editor enough detail to determine if the proposed book is suitable for her or his publishing program.

The proposal is now almost ready to be sent to the publisher. I say *almost* because, as was the case with the journal article, some homework must still be done. Once again, engage in strategic publishing. Peruse the recent catalogs of various publishers to determine if they publish books on your topic or area and if they publish the type of book you are proposing. You may wish to have your book published by a specific publisher because they have a strong reputation. But do they have a strong reputation for publishing books on your topic? Do they have a strong reputation for publishing scholarly monographs, or are they primarily a textbook publisher? Do they publish many edited volumes or do they prefer authored books? Unlike the journal manuscript, it is not unethical to send a book proposal to several publishers simultaneously, but these submissions should not be indiscriminate.

Regardless of which publishers are sent the proposal, before it goes out it should be proofread. Remember: you are trying to convince an editor that you are a good writer and a careful scholar. You may have impeccable credentials that establish your expertise on the topic on which you are writing, but if your proposal and vita have multiple typos and grammatical errors, you will not make a favorable impression on editors and reviewers.

A final word is in order about coauthored or coedited books. It is not a myth that many friendships have ended as a result of an attempt to cowrite or coedit a book. My impression is that the tension is less over who will have first authorship and more over the division of labor, or more accurately, fulfillment of the division of labor. Joint publishing ventures require that all those involved are clear on their responsibilities for the project and that they fulfill those responsibilities on time and to the best of their ability. Be sure *before* you agree to coauthor or coedit a book that you can work with the other individuals involved – that, quite simply, you get along with them – and that you can trust them to complete their assigned tasks just as they can trust you to complete yours.[8]

Conclusion

While publishing may be daunting, especially for those new to academe, it may be comforting to know that in some ways it gets easier as you do it more. Still, no matter how many publications you accrue on your vita, the basic "rules" I have presented in this chapter do not change. While I have attempted to address those aspects of journal and book publishing about which I receive the most questions, I am certain I have missed issues of concern to some authors. Consequently, I welcome queries from readers; if I don't know the answer to your question, chances are I can refer you to someone who does. In any event, I wish you success in your research and writing endeavors. As with anything worthwhile in life, publishing is challenging, but richly rewarding.

Notes

1 I am grateful to my colleague and friend, Denise Boots (University of Texas at Dallas) for the concept of "strategic publishing."

2 Incidentally, my answer to the first question is "It depends." *VAW*'s page limit for research articles is thirty-five double-spaced pages, all-inclusive of notes, references, tables, etc. If a manuscript is a bit over that limit, I encourage the author to submit it anyway; if it is more than ten pages over the limit, I ask the author to makes cuts before submitting it. My answer to the second question is Yes, but I also caution authors that I can make no guarantees regarding publication, since every manuscript must undergo peer review.

3 Proofreading really means checking the *printed* proofs for printer's errors but the term is used by analogy for this equally important earlier stage.

4 The peer-review process has been the subject of some intense criticism, with authors from diverse disciplines offering various recommendations for revising it. See, for example, Borer (1997), Fontaine (1995), Hunter (1995), and Staller (2007).

5 Although the discussion in this section focuses on scholarly monographs, much of the information pertains to textbooks as well. Although most publishers expect to see the information I cover here in a proposal, it is wise to also consult a publisher's web-site, since each posts information for prospective authors that gives their specifications for a book proposal. See, for example, http://www.routledge.com/info/authors, http://www.oup.co.uk/academic/authors/proposals/, and http://www.sagepub.com/publishwithsage.nav.

6 I must insert a note of gratitude at this point. To paraphrase a line I wrote in the preface to one of my books, if patience is a virtue, I have been blessed over the years with some incredibly virtuous editors. Among them are Gerhard Boomgaarden at Routledge, and Karen Hanson and Jeff Lasser at Allyn & Bacon. I thank them not only for their patience despite my tardiness on various projects, but also for their support and encouragement as I have weathered several small and not so small storms in my personal and professional lives.

7 Even when an edited book will comprise previously published work, prospective editors must consider the time it will take to obtain reprint permission from copyright holders. And reprint permission also entails the question of permission fees, which I have found to vary widely, depending on factors such as how recently the work was published, whether it was an academic or trade publication, and the celebrity of the author, in addition to the usual issues of the anticipated price of your book, the print run, and your intended audience. Your publisher will provide specific instructions on obtaining reprint permissions, but editors need to think through for the proposal how permission fees will be paid, since they can be a substantial expense. One common arrangement is for publishers to pay permission fees for the editor as an advance against royalties on the book. However, publishers will sometimes pay permission fees up to an agreed-upon amount, with costs in excess of that sum paid from the editor's royalties or directly by the editor. Certainly the payment of permission fees is a point of negotiation between book editors and publishers.

8 I have had the good fortune over the past fifteen years to have authored and edited books with some exceptionally smart and extraordinarily hard-working individuals, including Raquel Bergen (St. Joseph's University) and Jeff Edleson (University of Minnesota). I not only trust them to get the job done (and then some), but to do so with amazing good humor. I'm grateful for their willingness to keep working with me.

References

American Sociological Association (2009) *Publishing Options: An Author's Guide to Journals* (e-book), available for order from http://www.asanet.org.

Borer, D. A. (1997) "The ugly process of journal submissions: A call for reform," *Political Science and Politics*, 30: 558–60.

Fontaine, S. I. (1995) "With writers' eyes: Perception and change in manuscript review procedures," *Rhetoric Review*, 13: 259–64.

Frey, B. S. (2003) "Publishing as prostitution? Choosing between one's own ideas and academic success," *Public Choice*, 116: 205–23.

Germano, W. (2005) *From Dissertation to Book*, Chicago: University of Chicago Press.

Hunter, S. (1995) "The case for reviewing as collaboration and response," *Rhetorical Review*, 13: 265–72.

Robinson, A. (1988) "Thinking straight and writing that way: Publishing in *Gifted Child Quarterly*," *Gifted Child Quarterly*, 32: 367–69.

Staller, K. (2007) "Metalogue as methodology: Inquiries into conversations among authors, editors and referees," *Qualitative Social Work*, 6: 137–57.

7 Collaborating with practitioners

Carolyn Rebecca Block, Deshonna Collier-Goubil, Angela Moore and Winifred L. Reed

Do you remember why you first decided to make an academic career in your discipline? Was doing research that "makes a difference" one of your reasons? One way to make that happen is to form or join a collaboration with practitioners – community leaders, direct service providers and their agencies. And, we must admit that publishing is important to an academic career. To publish, you may need to have access to pertinent data, and that means working with the caretakers of those data – practitioners who maintain large archived datasets and direct service providers who collect and maintain client data. But just obtaining access to a dataset may not help you do research that is relevant to a community's needs, although you may get a publication out of it. To design and carry out relevant, high-quality research, you must thoroughly understand the meaning of the data. Collaboration with the practitioners who care for that data is a way to make that happen.

By collaborative research, we mean research conducted jointly by academic researchers and practitioners at every stage, from developing the initial idea, through designing and carrying out the research project, to analyzing and disseminating the results. Research partnerships and action research projects are not necessarily collaborations, although they may be. Research partnerships can range from a simple agreement for the agency to provide data to the researcher to a truly collaborative project. Action research projects are likely to be collaborations, or evolve to be collaborations, because they aim to help the community respond to a problem, but they also can be a simple partnership, not a true collaboration. A true collaboration fosters an environment where the researcher and practitioner work to develop shared goals, shared research and practice standards, a research agenda, and plans for data collection and dissemination (Block et al. 1999a, b). A "collaborative culture" (Block et al. 1999b) evolves, which encourages each collaborator, regardless of background, to contribute to both the research and practice aspects of the project. Each member of the group learns from and teaches others.

All four of us have worked for many years, in our individual careers, to develop and sustain research collaborations between academic researchers and practitioners. We have also been part of the growing Collaboration Working Group, a network of people who share their experiences and try to help each other develop and sustain truly collaborative research projects. In their network discussions and in the Collaboration Workshop that they have organized for four years at the American Society of Criminology meetings, the eighty Working Group members have accumulated a wealth of information.[1] As a group, the Collaboration Working Group has learned a lot about paths to successful collaborations, challenges, and barriers that can threaten collaboration, and roads to meeting those challenges and sustaining the collaboration. In this chapter, we hope to sum up that experience for you, to help you enter and negotiate the world of collaborative research.

Benefits of collaboration

Let's start with the reasons for researcher–practitioner collaboration, both your reasons and a practitioner's reasons. Why should you bother to build or join a collaboration? Why should practitioners want to collaborate with you? To build and sustain a successful collaboration, you must appreciate the perspectives of the collaborating practitioners in your collaboration. To do that, you need to be aware of both the potential benefits to them and the obstacles that they might face by joining a collaboration.

Benefits for academic researchers and their institutions

Socially relevant research goals. Practitioners' familiarity with the way things work in the real world will help the project team seek answers to questions that are most important to the community (Mouradian et al. 2001).

Increased quality of research. With the input of practitioners and clients with direct experience, researchers can learn to shape studies around the questions of those in the field. This in turn can increase research legitimacy and utility, since it is based on the experiences of study participants.

Enhanced study design. Practitioners can help academic researchers design a study that will address the questions that need to be answered. They have been trained to provide a host of services to diverse communities, and have learned a lot from and about the communities they serve. In addition, their work requires them to provide services that are culturally relevant, sensitive and appropriate.

Improved sample construction. Practitioners can help forge a sample design in which no one to whom the sample structure applies is systematically excluded. This is one of many challenges with research design (sampling bias, poor instrumentation, lack of control groups) that collaborative research can address (Jordan 2009). It is very difficult to design a sample that includes the voices of those who do not use mainstream services (Block 2004; Ford et al. 2002; Richie 1996), but the grassroots knowledge of practitioners can help overcome that challenge.

More effective procedures to protect subjects. Because practitioners often work with vulnerable populations, they are attuned to safety and confidentiality issues that academics may overlook and can help the collaboration design and carry out a safe, respectful, sensitive, and ethical project (Watts et al. 2001).

More relevant instruments. Practitioners' field-level expertise can guide the research project to a design that actually measures what the collaborators want to know, thus enhancing construct validity. In the Chicago Women's Health Risk Study (CWHRS), for example, the extensive collaboration on survey instruments produced questions that were relevant to the realities and risks in the lives of abused women and were written in culturally competent and nonjudgmental language (Block et al. 1999b).

Improved implementation of study findings. Practitioners' knowledge of the inner workings of complex organizations can help the collaborators examine multifaceted problems and evaluate the myriad responses to them. They may suggest interventions for the problems the study is addressing, or the best ways interventions can be implemented to maximize buy-in by an organization or community. Thus, collaborative research can enhance accountability to clients and the communities practitioners serve.

Increased service to the community. Does your institution require community service? Collaborative research is one way to provide it. Also, collaboration can improve your credibility in the community, laying the foundation for future studies. When a collaboration is able to provide research opportunities for undergraduate or graduate students, they can learn about collaboration methods and use their knowledge in their career. As a result, researcher–practitioner collaborations can improve the quality of science over time.

Benefits for practitioners and agencies

Better-quality research. Practitioners or agency staff may have wonderful data and may be asking important questions but lack the scientific training to design and conduct a study to answer those questions. In a collaborative project, researchers can make sure that the results of the study are valid and reliable.

Increased understanding of complicated issues. Academic researchers are trained to access and interpret the literature relevant to the topic at hand, and can search for, compile, and share it with the collaborative group. They can help the group identify practices that show promise but has not been rigorously evaluated, and those that evidence has demonstrated to be effective.

Data analysis. Academic researchers can help practitioners better understand the questions under consideration from an empirical perspective. They can transform complex problems or multifaceted programs into measurable variables.

Wider perspective. Just as practitioners' knowledge and perspective can help researchers design and carry out a better study, researchers can help shed light on issues that practitioners may not notice or may be unwilling to address (Riger 1990).

Positive institutional change. A collaborative research project can become a catalyst for change in the agency. The collaboration may unearth different ideas, processes and procedures that prove helpful to the agency in the long term. When practitioners have their specific questions answered, they may become more motivated to use research information to shape practice and to participate in future studies. The quality of programs and services practitioners provide may be enhanced as a result.

Collaborative skills

You have learned many things in your graduate education – how to write a research paper, how to study for an exam, even how to teach. You may not, however, have learned the interpersonal skills needed to form and sustain an effective collaboration. Both researchers and practitioners bring their technical expertise to the collaborative table, but that is not enough. Interpersonal skills are also critical (Knox and Lomonaco 2003). Below we outline some of the most important interpersonal skills underlying the successful development and maintenance of practitioner–researcher collaborations.

Communication. Collaboration requires effective communication, willingness to hear and listen by all parties (Fortuin and King 2007). Without effective communication, it will be difficult, if not impossible to engender trust. As we discussed above, researchers must understand what brings practitioners to the table, and practitioners must understand the goals of researchers. Reminding each other of "why we are here" is critical at every stage of the collaboration, because goals can change over time and because collaborations are sustained through challenging periods by remembering the fundamental reasons for the collaboration. Not only should collaborators clearly communicate their goals, they should communicate their expectations for each other's roles (Nyden et al. 1997b; Edleson and Bible 2001). And because these goals and expectations will evolve and change, everyone must work hard to keep the lines of communication open throughout the collaborative process.

Trust. True collaborations must be built upon trust. How difficult is it to write a dissertation if your dissertation chair does not trust you? How about being an assistant professor with a department chair who does not trust you? Trust follows from good communication. Practitioners should not assume that all researchers are "scientific and disinterested," although some may be. Researchers should not assume all practitioners have an "agenda," although some will.

Respect. When the collaborators establish good communication and trust, mutual respect can follow. Researchers must show that they value the importance and legitimacy of practitioner experience and expertise, and practitioners must show that they recognize the importance of research and accepted research practices. Everyone must respect each other's domain. Shared control of the research process, from jointly developing research questions to working together to disseminate study findings, helps tremendously to build respect, and encourages mutual respect and reciprocal learning. It also provides many opportunities for researchers to learn about practice and for practitioners to learn about research (Gondolf et al. 1997).

Honesty. It is vital to be realistic about what each party can and cannot contribute to a research collaboration. First, be honest with yourself. Closely examine the research and interpersonal skills you bring to the table and areas where you might need assistance. For example, researchers are trained to examine statistical relationships and evaluate interventions but may not be trained in policy analysis or advocating a course of action. Then, everyone should communicate clearly to the group the individual strengths and weaknesses of their individual training and experience. This kind of honesty can avoid many potential misunderstandings. Everyone will know what is expected of them. This will then lay a foundation for reciprocal learning, beginning to venture as a visitor into each other's worlds.

Commitment. Collaborations require a considerable amount of information exchange and learning. This never happens overnight, and the slow pace may sometimes be very frustrating to group members. In addition, the road to collaborative research is seldom smooth. There are often obstacles and barriers that might seem to threaten the very existence of the research collaboration. Such storms are more easily weathered when each collaborator knows why they and why everyone else came to the collaboration, and when everyone agrees on the ultimate goals of the research. Commitment provides the strength necessary to sustain the collaborative research. Remember to be patient with the process and with your fellow collaborators.

Shared standards. Successful collaborations work to develop shared goals and consensus on a few key practice and research standards. These shared standards become the foundation of the project and engender the trust necessary to accomplish the project's tasks and reach its goals (Block et al. 1999a,1999b). To develop project standards, make sure that your standards are clear and limited to a small number. Each collaborator must understand, support, and be able to explain to others and put into practice each standard, which is difficult with numerous or vague standards. Training researchers in practice issues and practitioners in research issues can help develop the mutual understanding and support necessary to reach consensus. Then be sure to allocate sufficient project time to come to an agreement about the standards, to continually reinforce their importance with the group, and to teach their importance to new members joining the collaboration. This foundation of your collaboration deserves a high priority in your time scheduling.

Willingness to teach, willingness to learn. In a true collaboration, all parties function as "co-researchers" (Block et al. 1999a, 1999b; Kondrat and Juliá 1997). Each member brings complementary and necessary skills to the project (Maguire 1987; Renzetti 1997). Reciprocal learning is a vital aspect of developing shared fundamental standards. Be sure that your collaboration provides many opportunities for researchers and practitioners to teach and learn from each other.

Barriers and pitfalls, and how to overcome them

Just as in any relationship, you will face ups and downs in your collaborations. To help you avoid barriers and pitfalls, or at least to be prepared for them, we offer the following suggestions. You will know that you have established a truly collaborative relationship when everyone's expertise and contributions are equally valued. How do you make that happen in a climate where researchers and practitioners live in different worlds with different perspectives, or may even be adversarial (Hufft 2005; Levin 1999)?

Blurred roles. Although permeable roles engender respect and are the foundation of building a collaborative culture, completely blurred roles can present a pitfall. This happens when one person feels the need to take over another person's role in the project. The best way to avoid this pitfall is to build respect and trust. People who trust each other are less likely to feel the need to take over the other's job. Also, be sure to maintain clear and open lines of communication. This way, if either party becomes uncomfortable with the others' boundaries, a conversation can dissolve this pitfall easily. Be careful, however, not to let fear of blurred roles get in the way of reciprocal learning and building respect. Allow room for collaborators to try on each other's shoes.

Divergent perspectives. As a researcher, you must be sensitive to the political and community environment of the research (Riger 1999). The exigencies of the work environment often lead practitioners to make quick decisions with incomplete information. It's not uncommon for them to say, "I want to know if my program works but I don't want to wait five years to find out." In addition, practitioners may be intimidated by the world of academia, and this intimidation may place constraints on their ability to participate freely in project discussions. In an all too common situation, practitioners can feel frustrated and disrespected if they have limited access to academic collaborators and must deal day-to-day with graduate students who have a high turnover and varied competence (Cunningham 2008). To avoid these pitfalls, the collaboration must nurture open communication and respect for all parties.

Differences in degree of institutional support. Unlike most academic researchers, a practitioner's job description seldom includes research. Although you may have funding to support your participation in a research collaboration, practitioners often do not. They must catch the time between other pressing and immediate responsibilities to work on a research project. Be aware of this inequality when you develop the project's timeline and budget, and make it the business of the collaborative project to equal the playing field whenever possible. Check with your institution to determine if you can contribute financial resources to the practitioner organization for this purpose, and ask the practitioner agency to underwrite the researcher's time spent in the collaboration.

Competing and conflicting goals. Practitioners who believe they were used for "drive-by" research may be reluctant to collaborate with any other researcher, and their attitude may influence their agency and their friends and colleagues. However, seemingly conflicting goals, such as gaining publications from the research project versus obtaining definitive and quick answers, can both be met with open communication and mutual trust. From the beginning of the project, researchers should be honest and upfront about their plans to publish the findings. The collaboration should build consensus about data dissemination over the course of the project.

Difficult results. When the data collection is over and the analysis begins to produce results, what do you do if the results are not what you expected, or put the practitioner's agency in a bad light? The first thing to do when results surprise or dismay is to make sure that the study was conducted appropriately. Given that the results are valid, they should be published. Avoid the temptation to provide "feel-good" results to practitioner agencies. This is not only disrespectful but will destroy the practitioner's trust in the honesty and expertise of the researcher. Similarly, when valid collaborative research results challenge accepted theory or previous research, publish them. Remember that research based on a good community sample and field-tested operationalization may not agree with research based on interviews of college students or a selected group of women in a shelter.

Collaborator turnover. When a researcher or practitioner leaves the project, the continuation of the collaboration can be threatened. Career moves are part of work life, and we must prepare ourselves for the possibility that a collaborator may take on a different position in the middle of our research. To overcome this barrier, try to protect and sustain your collaboration if at all possible. If a practitioner is moving, try to continue the collaboration for the good of the community. If you are moving, perhaps the collaboration can expand to your new university or setting. It can be very frustrating to have to start over from scratch, but the upside of things is that you now have a connection to a new agency. Be sure not to abandon the originating agency and communities, however. Make every effort to continue to work with them toward desired goals, but if sustaining is not an option, be sure to communicate the move as early in advance as possible.

Supporting the collaboration

Now that you know how to build and form a collaborative research relationship, you may be wondering how to maintain it. Some of the groundwork for sustaining a collaboration is laid from the first organizational meetings, but maintenance work must continue through all of the stages of collaboration (Elden 1981). Each stage has its own particular tasks, potential problems and barriers.

Initial organization of the collaboration. In the beginning, practitioners may think that because they are on the front-lines in responding to the needs of community members, they should set the research agenda. Researchers with extensive knowledge in a particular area may feel that they should make the research decisions. The first task, therefore, is to build consensus on the project's focus (intervention, basic research or a combination), the products to be developed as a result of the project, the timeline for products and major milestones, and basic research and safety standards. This consensus lays the foundation for the research project, and gives the collaboration the resilience necessary to withstand any future challenges to its existence.

A second task that your collaboration must confront early on is the project's division of labor. Researchers and practitioners must agree on their respective roles in the conceptualization, design, implementation, analysis, interpretation and dissemination of findings of the research. Who will have responsibility for maintaining the data and protecting confidentiality? Who will be responsible for protecting subjects' safety and identity? Will all collaborators have access to the data? Will the project's datasets be archived, and who will be responsible for that? What principles will govern data interpretation? Should the practitioners be able to approve the research results prior to any publication? If there is a conflict between interpretations of the results, what priorities will predominate? Who will do the publishing? How will the results be disseminated and to whom? Whose names will be listed as authors? Collaborators must work toward consensus on these issues, beginning with the first organizational meetings.

Seeking funding. Most collaborative projects must seek funding to carry out the research. Collaborate on the research proposal, work together to develop a budget that supports both the project and the collaborative process, and agree on how financial resources will be used. Try to build in enough financial support to cover the actual costs of each contributor, recognizing practitioner agencies as equal to other collaborators and being sure that they are compensated accordingly (Miedema 1996). If each collaborator takes the time to understand the other's world and perspective, including financial needs and constraints, the group can avoid a common complaint of helping agencies asked to provide data for research – that the researcher gets the money and the practitioner gets the work.

Research confidentiality, safety and ethics. Although you have undoubtedly completed at least one institutional review board (IRB) training by this point in your career, we must emphasize the profound ramifications for scientific inquiry of human subject protection. From the beginning, the collaboration must make clear to everyone that safety, privacy, and confidentiality are nonnegotiable. To the extent possible, the collaboration and the research project should do no harm. Be prepared for practitioners to inquire about your track record in dealing with safety and confidentiality in previous studies before they commit to the collaboration. If a researcher seems clueless, practitioners may look elsewhere.

The research process. Most practitioners have a clear stake in what research questions get asked, how they are asked, what the results show, and how the research project will benefit their organization and clientele. While they may not want to have responsibility for data collection or analysis, they do want an opportunity to review the research results and shed light on interpretation.

Many also want to be involved in disseminating the findings. Stephanie Riger (1999: 1105) argues that differences in result interpretation are "not simply one of different perspectives but, rather, the unequal positions and the relations among them that shape those perspectives." Do everything you can to remove this inequality. The collaborators themselves and the collaborating agencies should be the first to see the study results and drafts of publications.

Collaborators should develop a plan to handle negative research findings. We cannot stress this enough! Some practitioners embark upon evaluations of their programs to prove they work and can be devastated to discover that they were wrong. At the outset, therefore, the collaborators must broach the possibility for negative findings in group discussion. When all parties work together to build a solid strategy for moving forward if the study results in negative findings, later misunderstandings will be avoided.

Sustaining the collaboration. Because collaborations require continual maintenance to survive and because collaborations evolve over time, the requirements for supporting an existing research collaboration may differ from the requirements for building a collaboration. Challenges inevitably arise with each stage of the collaborative project. For example, you may find that collaboration maintenance exceeds the resources included in your proposal. As a collaborator, you must be committed to working through these challenges, since true collaboration is long term (Cunningham and Duffee 2007). Persist in working together to overcome barriers. Even when the initial collaborative project does not work out, remember that the collaborators have learned important lessons that can be applied to future collaborative projects.

Sustainable collaborations not only nurture current members but are also willing to add chairs to the table. Continuing participation is supported by taking care of the collaborators (Block et al. 1999a,1999b) – fostering mutual respect, encouraging permeable roles, and working hard to maintain communication. If possible, arrange face-to-face meetings on a regular basis, and hold them in both domains. You should attend staff meetings at practitioner organizations when possible and provide updates on the progress of the research. Similarly, practitioners should attend meetings at the researchers' offices so they can become familiar with the researchers' environments. Newcomers should be introduced respectfully to the rest of the group, socialized into the study goals and the agreed-upon practice and research standards, and brought up to date on project history. It is important to build and maintain an institutional memory, not only to socialize newcomers but also to remind current collaborators of how far the collaboration has come.

Conclusion

Collaborative research projects are conducted jointly by academic researchers and practitioners at every stage, from developing the initial idea, to designing and carrying out the research project, and analyzing and disseminating the results. They work by developing shared goals with consensus on a few key practice and research standards. Building and maintaining an academic–practitioner research collaboration requires continuing effort, flexibility, the investment of time and resources, and willingness to think outside of the traditional academic or practitioner box. However, this investment relationship can produce great rewards.

In a true collaboration, both researchers and practitioners learn to enter each other's worlds and to appreciate each other's perspectives. This not only improves the quality of the research but is an opportunity for all collaborators to learn valuable life lessons. As a collaborative culture develops and the researcher–practitioner roles begin to blur, practitioners develop a greater understanding and appreciation of the practicality of research methods. At the same time, you will build a deeper understanding of the grassroots implications of practitioners' theories and begin to hear the voices of the people you are studying together.

Note

1 This chapter builds upon the presentations and discussions at the four Collaboration Workshops held at the American Society of Criminology, and on the lively and informative discussions of participants in the Collaboration Working Group Forum. We especially appreciate the contributions of Joanne Belknap, who has worked with us over the years to summarize the key points raised in those discussions.

References

Block, Carolyn Rebecca (2004) "Risk factors for death or life-threatening injury for abused women in Chicago," in Bonnie Fisher (ed.) *Violence against Women and Family Violence: Developments in Research, Practice, and Policy* (NCJ 199731, November),Washington, DC: National Institute of Justice, http://beta.nij.ncjrs.org/vawprog/drpp/sec1.html.

Block, Carolyn Rebecca, Barbara Engel, Sara Naureckas, and Kim Riordan (1999a) "Collaboration in the Chicago Women's Health Risk Study," *Research Brief*, 1 (1), June. Chicago: Illinois Criminal Justice Information Authority.

Block, Carolyn Rebecca, Barbara Engel, Sara Naureckas, and Kim Riordan (1999b) "The Chicago Women's Health Risk Study: Lessons in collaboration," *Violence Against Women*, 5 (10), October: 1158–77.

Cunningham, Scott (2008) "Voices from the field: Practitioner reactions to collaborative research initiatives," *Action Research*, 6 (4): 373–90.

Cunningham, Scott, and David E. Duffee (2007) *Dilemmas in Child Welfare Partnerships: Sustaining Engagement for the Long Run*, Atlanta, GA: American Society of Criminology.

Edleson, Jeffry L., and Andrea L. Bible (2001) "Collaborating for women's safety: Partnerships between research and practice," in Claire M. Renzetti, Jeffrey L. Edleson, and Raquel Kennedy Bergen (eds) *Sourcebook on Violence against Women*, Thousand Oaks, CA: Sage, 73–96.

Elden, Maxwell (1981) "Sharing the research work: New role demands for participative researchers," in Peter Reason and John Rowan (eds) *Human Inquiry: A Sourcebook of New Paradigm Research*, London: Wiley, 253–66.

Ford, David A., Ronet Bachman, Monika Friend, and Michelle Meloy (2002) *Controlling Violence against Women: A Research Perspective on the 1994 VAWA's Criminal Justice Impacts*, Washington, DC: National Institute of Justice, U.S. Department of Justice.

Fortuin, Betty, and Erica King (2007) *Practitioner, Researcher and Government Official: Do we Speak the Same Language?*, Atlanta, GA: American Society of Criminology.

Gondolf, Edward W., Kersti Yllo, and Jacquelyn C. Campbell (1997) "Collaboration between researchers and advocates," in G. K. Kantor and Janice Jasinski (eds) *Out of Darkness: Contemporary Research Perspectives on Family Violence*, Thousand Oaks, CA: Sage, 255–67.

Hufft, Anita G. (2005) *Cultural Dissonance: Challenges to Collaboration in Correctional Health Care Research*, Toronto, Ont.: American Society of Criminology.

Jordan, Carol E. (2009) "Advancing the study of violence against women: Evolving research agendas into science," *Violence Against Women*, 15 (4), April: 393–419.

Knox, Lyndee, and Carmela Lomonaco (2003) *Recognizing and Nurturing Collaborative Skills in a Practice-based Research Network*, Denver, CO: American Society of Criminology.

Kondrat, Mary Ellen, and Maria Juliá (1997) "Participatory action research: Self-reliant research strategies for human social development," *Social Development Issues*, 19 (1): 32–49.

Levin, Rebekah (1999) "Participatory evaluation: Researchers and service providers as collaborators versus adversaries," *Violence Against Women*, 5 (10): 1213–27.

Maguire, Patricia (1987) *Doing Participatory Research: A Feminist Approach*, Amherst, MA: Center for International Education, School of Education, University of Massachusetts.

Miedema, Baukje (1996) "Building a research team: The struggle to link the community and the academy," *Atlantis*, 20 (2): 89–93.

Mouradian, Vera E., Mindy B. Mechanic, and Linda M. Williams (2001) *Recommendations for Establishing and Maintaining Successful Researcher–Practitioner Collaborations*, Wellesley, MA: National Violence Against Women Prevention Research Center.

Nyden, Philip, Anne Figert, Mark Shibley, and Darryl Burrows (1997a) *Building Community Social Science in Action*, Thousand Oaks, CA: Sage.

Nyden, Philip, Anne Figert, Mark Shibley, and Darryl Burrows (1997b) "University–community collaborative research: Adding chairs at the research table," in Phil Nyden, Anne Figert, Mark Shibley, and Darryl Burrows (eds) *Building Community: Social Science in Action*, Thousand Oaks, CA: Sage, 3–13.

Renzetti, Claire M. (1997) "Confessions of a reformed positivist: Feminist participatory research as good social science," in Martin D. Schwartz (ed.) *Researching Sexual Violence against Women: Methodological and Personal Perspectives*, Thousand Oaks, CA: Sage, 131–43.

Richie, Beth E. (1996) *Compelled to Crime: The Gender Entrapment of Battered Black Women*, New York: Routledge.

Riger, Stephanie (1990) "Ways of knowing and community–organizational research," in P. Tolan, C. Keys, F. Chertok, and L. Jason (eds) *Researching Community Psychology: Integrating Theories and Methodologies*, Washington, DC: American Psychological Association.

Riger, Stephanie (1999) Guest editor's introduction to "Working together: Challenges in collaborative in research on violence against women," *Violence Against Women,* 5 (10): 1099–117.

Watts, Charlotte, Lori Heise, and Mary Ellsberg (2001) *Putting Women's Safety First: Ethical and Safety Recommendations for Research on Domestic Violence against Women,* Geneva: Department of Gender and Women's Health, World Health Organization, http://www.who.int/gender/violence/womenfirtseng.pdf.

8 Getting tenure and redressing denial

Kristine Mullendore

For what are typically the first six years of your academic career you will essentially be on probation, working towards obtaining tenure under some sort of continuing or renewable employment contract. If you are not awarded tenure by the end of that sixth year, your job is gone within a year and you have a limited set of options that include: (1) challenging the denial through the institution's grievance process in hopes of obtaining tenure so that you may stay; (2) if you can prove that your employment rights were violated in the tenure process, you can file a lawsuit requesting the award of damages and a court order giving you the tenure status that you were denied; and (3) you can update your curriculum vitae and use your remaining year of employment to find a new position. Possessing a complete understanding of tenure and its processes is of critical importance to both your becoming tenured and deciding what you should do in the event that you do not.

Tenure and the tenure process

Tenure

Tenure is a twentieth-century concept that was created to protect senior university faculty rights to intellectual and academic freedom as well as to protect them from arbitrary and unfair administrative actions of dismissal and demotion (Adams 2006; Dekat 2009;). As Cloud notes, "Tenured faculty enjoy the expectation and privilege of continuing employment unless the institution can demonstrate good cause to terminate their appointment. In principle, tenure is not a guarantee of lifetime employment; it is a promise of due process in dismissal" (Cloud 1998: 931).

Historically, obtaining tenure status provided the same job security that existed at that time in nonacademic work settings; however, while job security no longer exists in a wider context, academic tenure continues to be a part of academic work environments in the twenty-first century despite its critics (Helms et al. 2001). A junior faculty member's pursuit of this tenure status has been compared to the pursuit of the Holy Grail or Golden Fleece (Adams 2006; Shea 2002). That is because it is simultaneously a symbol of success in your profession and a validation of your worth, reflecting that you have received external recognition in your chosen field, that you satisfy its academic requirements (Moody 2000).

Another reason that tenure is a critical point of transition in your academic life is because it inverts your employment status. This status guarantees economic security, your right to due process in any employment action filed against you, and provides academic freedom to do "unfettered intellectual work, and the ability to determine their research agenda" that is essential to your future academic life (Austin and Rice 1998: 1). Pretenure, you have the burden of periodically proving your value to the institution in order to justify keeping your job. Once granted tenure, that burden shifts from you to the institution and also changes into an institutional obligation to continue your employment, unless just cause can be shown for terminating that tenure. Tenure ends your high level of uncertainty of continued employment as an "at-will" employee and eliminates your need to devote time and effort needed to comply with the renewal and tenure requirements and processes of your institution.

Along with the benefits of tenure come responsibilities. It is expected that faculty members will express independent opinions that influence and inform administrative decisions about resource allocations and other economic issues that impact the institution's research and educational mission. Senior faculty members with tenure can act more freely than junior faculty in presenting opposing or differing opinions from those of the administration on important academic issues involving curriculum, research and scholarly activity, and academic integrity concerns because they are less likely to face retaliatory actions by administrators (Nelson 1997). Once you are tenured you will take on this responsibility and the tenure process is also intended to prepare you for this role (Finkin and Post 2009).

However, becoming tenured and promoted is not an ineluctable result of your being hired, especially for women. The rates at which faculty achieve tenure can vary dramatically from institution to institution, depending on the type of the institution and its mission (Dekat 2009). Whether or not there is a good "fit" between your institution's expectations for your work life and your own expectations is something that should be carefully examined when you are deciding whether or not to accept a job offer. You should know both what the hiring institution expects of you in order for you to become tenured as well as have information about its tenure procedures. The traditional areas of responsibility for faculty at institutions of higher education include teaching, researching and publishing, and the performance of service to your institution, community, and the larger discipline. The importance and value given to each of these areas, however, differs widely according to the nature and mission of each institution, as do their review processes and policies. For example, the relative importance of research and teaching is reversed between institutions who have a research-oriented mission (research being of most importance) and liberal arts institutions with a mission to provide excellence in undergraduate education (teaching undergraduates being of much more importance at these latter institutions). Understanding an institution's expectations for tenure is further complicated because the interests of the people who decide to be academics vary as widely in the nature of their disciplines and their scholarly work as do the domains of human knowledge. This variety results in institutional standards that are written in order to accommodate this large variety and faculty reviewers who apply these standards within the lens of their own disciplinary expertise. The combination of these two aspects alone accounts for much of the ambiguity present in the tenure process. Studies show, however, that there is one important characteristic that is shared across the disciplines; you are all passionate about your work and start your first academic position enthusiastic about creating and sharing knowledge with others; given the time and effort needed to earn your degrees, perhaps this is not surprising (Austin and Rice 1998). One caution, though: do not let that passion to obtain your first job and your desire to begin to engage in your academic life undermine the importance of being selective about where that occurs.

You should take into consideration your own individuality. If you love to teach and be in the classroom, you should make certain that this work is something that will be valued by your institution during your future tenure review processes. Conversely, if you are primarily interested in being a researcher and scholar, having no real interest in teaching in an undergraduate classroom, then you should not take a position at any institution expecting you to be significantly engaged in teaching this type of course. In a tough job market, any job may seem desirable, but you risk experiencing extreme difficulties in your initial job if your expectations are a poor "fit" with those of your institution. You will also be more likely to be unsuccessful in obtaining tenure and face an increased possibility that you could have to overcome any stigma that may attach if that should happen at your first academic position. A poor fit of your expectations, abilities, and interests with your university's expectations can result in your being subjected unnecessarily to increased daily stress at work as well as having a greater potential of exposing you to the emotional trauma, stigma, and other difficulties that can be caused by any critical tenure review assessment and tenure denial. When you accept a position, you need to have the best possible understanding that you can achieve about what their expectations are for you to receive tenure and whenever possible choose a position where those expectations align with your interests and abilities.

As a savvy tenure candidate, you should also act to reduce the levels of stress intrinsic to the process by converting it to the degree possible into one that has both developmental and promotional functions. By regularly seeking out and being receptive to your colleagues' opinions as to your performance, you gain important access to their opinions that allows you to respond to, and appropriately address, any legitimate concerns. Review processes that are both formative (developmental) and summative (evaluative) have the best results for you and your institution. Unsuccessful tenure processes are equally the failure of you and your institution. Any tenure process that results in a civil lawsuit is not a good result for either party, regardless of who prevails in any litigation. For your institution, the human capital you and your colleagues represent is its most important resource. It allocates significant financial resources to recruit, hire, train, and develop you, and your ultimate success is an equally shared and desired outcome. However, the tenure system places the burden of establishing compliance with its standards on you. Therefore, you should assume responsibility for the process being successful as if it were your sole responsibility. There are many resources that you can use to gain a good understanding of acknowledged good institutional practices that you can employ, especially if your institution does not recommend any in particular. Dr. Peter Seldin is one recognized expert in this area, and familiarizing yourself with his recommendations about how to present yourself in your tenure materials and how institutions may construct their faculty review processes is well worth your time (Seldin 2006; Seldin and Miller 2008).

The most central attributes and aspects of the tenure process that you should address over which you can have some control and influence are: establishing good communications; creating adequate documentation of events in appropriate forms as you move through the process; advocating for your interests and research agenda within your academic department; developing human relations skills and an understanding of organizational culture within your department; and networking to influence the opinions of faculty colleagues to improve their perceptions of a good "fit" with the institutional/departmental requirements.

Whatever process is used by your institution, it will at some point involve some type of "performance assessment" (whether formative or summative) by faculty colleagues and/or external reviewers and that process includes a component that is substantially subjective (Copeland and Murray 1996). Typically, tenure processes call for your initial performance assessment to be made by the other faculty members at the department level – your daily faculty work group. This decision will then be reviewed and approved, or reversed, by higher levels of administration. The personnel policies of each institution determine which faculty members are eligible to participate and vote in this process. At some institutions, administrators have a greater role in the initial determination than at others and at many institutions only tenured faculty are eligible to make these decisions. Regardless of who is eligible to participate and vote in the initial assessments and decisions, and whatever degree of variance exists as to whether these initial assessments are "honored" or "overruled" by higher reviewing administrators, it is usually the members of your closest work group that first render these judgments – your departmental colleagues. The reason given for deferring to this level of decision making is the recognition that each discipline has a unique set of knowledge and expertise and those who are outside of this area of specialization have great difficulty in assessing the performance of that tenure track candidate (Dekat 2009). Institutions find this specialization desirable in part because they are "selling" your specialized knowledge, along with the general knowledge of the discipline, to its students

(Siow 1998). However, the subjective nature of this peer assessment is often one of the principal sources of ambiguity for you in an already ambiguous process.

Another important aspect of academic life that you should understand is that academic institutions customarily operate under some form of a shared governance system. These shared governance systems are part of the reason why personnel review processes require multiple evaluators and multiple layers of decision making. Because of these multiple decision makers and review layers, there are increased possibilities for diverse opinions regarding the quality of your performance. This layered review process creates real possibilities of your having an initial department decision altered if the college level personnel committee does not endorse it. That college-level decision could be changed yet again since the dean, who has the appointing authority, and the Provost/President/Board of Trustees (Control) of the institution have the authority to change the decision when it reaches them (Franke 2000; Sawislak 1999). Even where the decisions at each level consistently approve your tenure, you will still be waiting for the end result and be aware that, until the process is concluded, no decision is final.

Thus, "negotiating tenure" includes for you two related, though significantly different, aspects both of which can significantly impact your experience. As discussed earlier, it first refers to the hiring negotiations that you engaged in that can set more specific and explicit terms for your performance expectations, establish your professional obligations to the institution and any reciprocal support obligations it commits to at the point of hire. Second, "negotiating tenure" refers to your journey as you find your path through the formal and informal environment of your institution and department. If the complexities of the formal review process are not enough, there are also the informal sets of expectations that can complicate the review process and be a hidden minefield of destruction.

Problems

The degree of stress and anxiety that you will experience in the tenure review process is difficult for anyone to understand who is outside the realm of higher education. Such movies as *D.O.A.* (1988) in which a senior tenured faculty member is killed by a junior faculty member because the senior member holds knowledge that could jeopardize the junior member's getting tenure are relatively unbelievable stretches of imagination unless you have been employed in an institution of higher education. The ambiguities intrinsic to the review process are principal sources of this stress. In addition, that you have no job security beyond your current contract or no guarantee that you will succeed in obtaining tenure are additional sources of stress. The criteria used to determine how well you are progressing over your probationary years in meeting your department's expectations are vague and there are few, if any, clear guidelines as to how to manage your efforts to satisfy their institutional and departmental expectations. Stress is the almost inevitable result.

It is at the time of the application of your institution's values to your work during the tenure review process that any problems that you may have complying with those standards will be revealed (Copeland and Murray 1996). This is especially true because your rights to academic freedom must also be added into the equation, so minimal guidance will be provided to you as you make your research and scholarship choices. Because of the unique nature of all faculty members' individual skills and accomplishments, the standards of review are written so as to be able to encompass and accommodate you and every other department candidate's unique characteristics. A decision that tenure should be given to you means that they have determined not only that there is a good "fit" between the institution and you, but also between you and your department's disciplinary perspective. Your department's initial decision to hire you can be analogized to choosing to buy a pair of shoes; whether that fit is really good can really only be assessed after the shoes have been worn for a while. If there wasn't a good fit at the point of hiring that will very soon become apparent. However, the tenure process is a "wearing" one, in part because of the ongoing choices you will make in your academic work and research as it develops over your probationary years, pretenure. These choices can result in your not being awarded tenure (with the consequent devastating effect on your future as an academic), even when your essential worth as an academic is not a cause of the decision – but rather only the lack of a "fit" between you and the department.

Formal performance expectations can place competing and conflicting demands on your time and this is another point of stress as you attempt to comply with them. Administrative efforts to "interpret" the evaluation criterion for you often exacerbate that tension; especially when those interpretations are also vague, internally inconsistent, and sometimes even conflict with the written statements of expectations for successful performance that are being interpreted. An example of this is where your institution has a written statement of performance expectations that include service to the university and community but you are informed by a departmental chair and/or colleague not to be concerned because service will not get you tenure. You are left to wonder if that means that service is not valued at all and you do not need to be concerned about that criterion. If that's true, though, then why is it a stated performance expectation? What happens if you follow that departmental level advice and then your performance is questioned because of your lack of compliance during the review conducted at higher levels? What impact will it have on your colleagues' or department chair's evaluation of you if you don't follow that advice? This is only one illustration of how your progress to tenure can be undermined by informal organizational culture and social environments that do not reflect institutional imperatives. Your uncertainty will naturally increase as you face any conflicting sets of expectations caused by the multilevel review process.

If your institution provides a formal periodic review process, you should take full advantage of it and use that process to obtain the peer assessment of your performance that you need to make good choices as you move through the tenure process. Be open to your colleagues' comments and suggestions. Use this review process as an opportunity to develop mentoring relationships whenever the senior faculty member is open to establishing those relationships. If your institution, as is too often the case, does not provide a formal method to obtain peer review input assessing your performance on an ongoing and regular basis, you should seek it out informally and before it is too late to alter your choices. Sometimes this can be a difficult task because the daily social interactions within your department which could naturally lead to this type of informal review are undermined by the absence of a formal structure for this input. This is especially true where the lack of formal structure is part of a social context where everyone knows that the tenure review process will inevitably require them to make this evaluation and that it is looming in the not too distant future. Without certainty in structured processes to fulfill peer review obligations, the chances of your department having the type of safe environment where informal exchanges of information concerning your performance that are essential to your success are less likely to occur – making it even more important for you to actively seek them out. These informal reviews also encourage your intellectual development, can support teaching development, and ensure that you receive feedback on whether the amount of time spent fulfilling your service obligations is excessive, something that should be of particular concern for female faculty, who often perform more service than male faculty colleagues.

How many faculty members successfully achieve tenure varies from institution to institution. At some institutions most tenure track faculty are successful. At others, it is a much riskier process. If you are a new faculty member at the most prestigious institutions the pressure on you will be especially strong. Knowing that some of these institutions rarely, if ever, grant tenure can significantly impact your performance (Fogg 2004). Even if there wasn't so much at stake for you, tenure processes create high levels of tension. However, pressure from scholarship requirements has intensified for junior faculty regardless of the prestige of your institution because the bar for success has been raised across the nation, at both research and teaching institutions. Universities which used to require the publication of one book, such as Columbia University, now require two, and teaching institutions needing to ensure high levels of student enrollment that want to enhance the profile of their institution have raised the scholarship level required for tenure (Wilson 2001). This increased level of scholarship expectation potentially has some corollary impacts that can complicate your review process. One such complication is that senior faculty evaluators reviewing your materials are evaluating, and possibly criticizing your performance as to either the quality or quantity of your work, when at the time of their tenure decision they did not have to meet the same high standards that they are now applying. Raised expectations can also result in your deciding to take what can be described as the "two-boxes" approach to assembling your portfolio materials for review. If more is required of you and quantity is at all important, then you are tempted to put everything in – increasing your work in assembling and organizing your review materials, and also increasing the work of senior faculty reviewers who must then wade through it all (Wilson 2001). Be careful to be appropriately selective and to present your materials so that you will be seen in the best light. If senior faculty feel unduly and unnecessarily burdened by the way you present yourself, there can be significant, even if "informal," negative impact on their assessments of your performance.

Even if it is true for your institution that almost everyone who applies for tenure receives it, the tenure process often has a hazing overtone to it that is not consistent with working in a safe and supportive environment. There can also be a "feeling" among senior faculty members that if they had to comply with these processes undergoing the anxiety and uncertainty, so should the present candidates, even though such attitudes are not conducive to creating a well-functioning academic department.

These reviewers necessarily devote a significant amount of time and effort to your personnel review, and they must have a formal and informal commitment to the process for it to be completely successful, both at the time of the formal review processes and during the daily interactions within your department (Szeto and Wright 2003). The formal process requires senior faculty to provide a "candid evaluation, a willingness to make hard decisions even about close colleagues, and personal investment in a sound institutional process" (Franke 2001: 1). Informally, it requires that senior faculty interact with junior faculty communicating to them the information they need on a daily basis as they engage in their "professoriate," so that the final tenure decision, favorable or unfavorable, is not a surprise. If it is a surprise to you, that is one good indication that the process may not have functioned as it should. Processes that lead to "realistic expectations and transparency" are critical to performance evaluation processes (Szeto and Wright 2003: 2).

Collegiality is a central concern in discussions of academic tenure. Collegiality encompasses determining how a junior faculty member will interact with colleagues in the future, based on past conduct (Mawdsley 1999). Even where it is not specifically identified as an institutional criterion for review, courts have upheld its consideration in the tenure process as an aspect of both teaching and service (Mawdsley 1999; Zirkel 1999). One of the toughest challenges you will face as a junior faculty member is managing your daily interactions with other faculty, particularly senior faculty, and the consequent impact on your future tenure and promotion evaluations. You should be aware, as Douglas and George note, that "All your achievements aren't worth a hill of chalk if your senior colleagues hate you" (Douglas et al. 2000: B10). Having a divisive relationship with either fellow colleagues or students can be a reason for non-renewal or tenure denial, even though it cannot be used as a pretext or camouflage for a personnel action that was the product of inappropriate discrimination (Mawdsley 1999).

Collegiality plays such a central role because personnel decisions are typically reached through a shared faculty governance approach. For personnel concerns, this means that the tasks of hiring (recruitment and selection) and evaluation of faculty are given to faculty, while the tasks of planning and resource allocation (creating a faculty line to be filled and providing university support for curriculum) is the province of administrators (Moody 2000). That the "professoriate" has the responsibility of determining these issues is, in fact, one aspect of the academic freedom that tenure is designed to protect (Williams 1999). The importance of collegial relations is also reinforced by the faculty governance processes. Newly tenured faculty members will have to be able to work within this governance system in a cooperative manner (Mawdsley 1999).

Female faculty members face subtle discrimination, even in our politically correct world where overt discrimination is avoided. Subtle discrimination can include having a hidden double standard, creating a higher bar for female candidates, having the value of their research questioned, or being told that they do not fit as a colleague because they are aggressive or difficult to get along with (Wagner 1991). Collegiality concerns often influence peer assessment of a new faculty member, as will be discussed later. Female faculty members face unique concerns in this area because when they speak up and make suggestions they are often perceived as not being collegial (Bellas 1999). Another problem for female faculty members is that tenure review processes are essentially promotions of self, a process that is easier for most men than for most women (Bellas 1999).

Another identifiable group of new faculty that experiences additional stress consists of faculty members with an interest in becoming parents; additional stress is created by the conflicting demands placed on their time. For the female faculty included within this group, the forces of aging create biological stress that can force a choice between spending time needed to meet tenure requirements or becoming a parent. The facetious statement by two commentators that "adoption remains an attractive option" is painfully pertinent to the dilemma faced by these women (Douglas and George 2000: B10).

New faculty members of color have unique concerns that need to be included in the creation of any mentoring network along with those of their female colleagues. Bonner, an associate professor of adult and higher education at the University of Texas in San Antonio, notes that the experiences of academic African-Americans cause them to believe that: they must constantly prove themselves; they will face organizational behavior that excludes them from professional networks requiring them to both conform to the culture of their academic department and face daily tension of moving between two social worlds; they are not welcomed by their department members, and they must put up with the status quo as they are unable to change the current system within which they work (Bonner 2004). Any new faculty member of color will need to seek out mentoring from senior faculty willing to assist them to avoid being isolated and to help support them.

Graduate programs provide new faculty members with differing degrees of mentoring and differing forms of socialization about what it means to be an academic. As mentioned in chapter1, graduate school mentoring is important for success in graduate schools (Bogat and Redner 1985). The importance of mentoring in professional employment is not clearly established, which may be because the ways in which mentoring occurs after employment differ from the mentoring done in graduate school, or it could be because institutional support for that relationship varies. However, the impact of mentoring in graduate schools and its continuing effects is well established in many disciplines (Bogat and Redner 1985). There are gender-based differences in the ability to obtain mentoring, creating concerns unique to new female faculty (Pedriolo 2004).

Solutions

The tenure path carries with it much potential for conflict, miscommunication, and imposes a high degree of stress on all the parties involved, but most particularly on you. It is in your best interests to work within, and with, your institution to anticipate and avoid the potential conflicts created by these ambiguous institutional expectations from the moment of hiring. If you begin from the first day with a sound understanding of the basic contract and employment law aspects of the tenure process and take these aspects into consideration as you advance towards tenure and promotion, you can avoid, or minimize, many of its hazards while also reducing conflict and the potential stigma that attaches to negative decisions.

To repeat, before taking a faculty position, you should obtain as much information as possible about your institution's tenure process. That information should include the tenure performance expectations (departmental, college, and university), timing and frequency of personnel reviews, the processes under which the review will occur, who the decision makers are (the eligible faculty voters), who has the appointment authority (typically the dean of the college), and the balance of decision-making authority as it is distributed between the academic department, college review committee, and any university-wide review committee.

Because institutions vary in their use of the four methods of evaluation – self-assessment, peer evaluations, supervisory evaluations, and student evaluations – you need to understand your institution's balance and then be able to communicate effectively your own performance. This includes being able to interpret and react to the input of others and actively solicit all necessary input that is essential to the assessment of all four of these areas of performance expectation.

Just as the reviewing faculty should be inclusive and sensitive to these concerns in their assessment of the candidates under review, the candidates also need to be sensitive to the need to advocate for themselves and improve the inclusivity of their departments by seeking out allies and mentors who can assist them in negotiating through these differences. This can be more difficult for women faculty than for their male colleagues.

Your conception of what is valued must align with the department's. It is here that gender issues and cultural variations in what should be valued can cause problems for faculty who are more diverse than the colleagues who will be reviewing their performance. Women faculty report feeling isolated, experience more stress and have more difficulty in establishing a mentoring relationship, and also experience negative evaluations when they advocate for, or promote, themselves (Steinpreis et al. 1999). This problem was recognized by the Association of American Colleges as early as 1993, when they published a guide to assist female faculty undergoing the tenure process containing many of the same practical recommendations being made here (Sandler 1992).

It is incumbent upon you to know the routes, methods, and timing, of communications regarding your tenure and renewal process (to anticipate the dates of review and consider them as you allocate your efforts to fulfill workload expectations on a daily and weekly basis). You also need to know what evaluative documents you will have to provide concerning your performance at the institution. Much of this information as to the formal processes will be detailed in faculty and/or employee handbooks produced by the institution. These are often provided to you upon your arrival at the institution, but can also be made available by your department chair, college dean, or posted in an electronic form to a university website. It is important that you check these at all levels of your institution, as university expectations are often explained with more specificity to the disciplines found within the colleges and then again within the departments of each college. Do not set aside these documents to read too much after initial series of orientation programs regarding the ways and culture of your institution are completed and the busy work of beginning a term is completed. You should seek out information about such mundane things as whether or not your university, college, or department maintains records of faculty involvement and presence at institutional events and the consequences of the failure to attend as expected, and, in the absence of affirmative knowledge of it carrying a neutral value, you should attend these events. Knowing what activities are going to be valued by those who will evaluate your performance allows you to make better choices about what events to attend and what committees or other working groups to join. The assignment to most university work occurs at the beginning of terms and the commitments made often cannot be altered, or at least not without creating another opportunity for negative impressions. Once you begin committee work, it is also important to remember that the other members of the group will be assessing you from the initial meetings. It is important to know what will count and what will not be valued.

One of the best ways to learn about a department and university's communication and documentation processes is to look at tenure materials created in the past. You should affirmatively seek out mentorship from more senior faculty members, if there is no formal assignment method at your institution.

You should request access to their contract renewal and tenure portfolios and review materials and examine these early upon arrival at your institution. Negative personnel decisions are often based on misguided choices about where to place your efforts that cannot be corrected after the fact.

If you find departmental expectations ambiguous, you should do everything you can to clarify them. If written standards do not exist, request them. If none are forthcoming, then speak to senior faculty members and others about what is expected and send a confirming email describing the understanding of the process that resulted from these conversations, while also thanking them for their assistance and time. These types of written statements are useful both in assuring your own understanding of what was said to you and as explanations at some later point in time for the choices you made about your workload allocation and the reasons behind your decisions. It will certainly make it more difficult for that particular faculty member to defensibly cast a negative vote on your personnel action, if you have met that stated expectation.

It also establishes a communication process in which your interest in having this type of feedback is established and creates the possibility of an ongoing discussion of your successes and shortcomings in achieving the goals for tenure set by the institution. It creates the type of atmosphere where you can be easily approached by other members of the faculty as to any areas of expectation you need to improve and can only operate to your advantage, eliminating later unpleasant surprises within your review process.

However, as with any communication, the form of the communication is often a critical factor in its effectiveness. Email and written statements are not always the best ways to interact with fellow faculty. Where you intend to engage in a dialogue with another person the conversation should be held face to face. It is only when you are engaging in such activities as seeking confirmation that your understanding of the concern discussed is correct that it should be reduced to writing. You should maintain hard copy and electronic records of all written communications regarding your performance. These records are useful for ensuring accuracy of the candidate's understanding of, and efforts to meet the department and institutional standards.

You should know yourself better than anyone. Whenever you take a job it is your responsibility to represent yourself well. You should pay attention to what happens when the group is together. You should pay attention to what behavior is wanted, valued, and expected from new faculty and attempt, within the limits of your conscience and own interests, to comply. As a new PhD you should be aware that senior faculty will be less impressed with your degree than you are. Adapting to the culture of a group is a difficult process and one that requires your overt attention.

You can be certain that senior faculty colleagues will be making a judgment concerning you at some defined future point(s). Academic work that supports your organization will be an important quality; however, making certain that others are aware of the value you bring to the organization is of even more importance. This is not a time for false modesty. In addition to the notification impact that occurs by letting others know of your research efforts and publication successes, you can also receive support and assistance in those efforts. The department chair, and administrators above the department, should be given the opportunity to support your development and contribute to your success. They are often the first point of contact for research and scholarship opportunities. If they are not fully aware of your plans and research agenda, they may not be able to support them fully – especially in this day of harsh economic times and dwindling resources. On a day-to-day basis, department heads are asked to provide names of persons in their departments with the expertise needed to assist in solving some problem either within or outside of the institution. You need to do what you can to make certain that the administrator directs those whom you can assist to you. This also contributes to their knowledge of your success as an ongoing measure, rather than only at the predetermined points of review.

Redressing denial of tenure

When your employment contract is not renewed, or you are denied tenure or promotion, you have three options: your institution's grievance processes, hiring a lawyer and filing a civil lawsuit challenging the decision, or looking for a new position. Because there are often very short time frames restricting when you may file a grievance, you should already know the formal and informal grievance processes of your institution in order to maintain your ability to file the grievance. When used appropriately, grievance processes can resolve the underlying conflicts while creating a more positive work environment for you, if you end up being successful in having the tenure denial overturned.

You can still turn to the U.S. court system, if you subsequently determine that is the best option for you or if you are unsuccessful in filing a grievance; however, any decision to file a lawsuit should be made with a good understanding of the risks and costs involved in these adjudicative processes. As a potential litigant, you should be certain that that is the best approach for you and ultimately that decision requires consultation with legal counsel. Short of you having strong proof that there has been a breach of your employment contract that included a failure to comply with institutional tenure process requirements or proof that there has been unlawful discrimination against you resulting in the violation of your constitutional or civil rights, it is rarely in either the candidate's or the institution's interests for the process to become so adversarial that it ends with you asserting that "I'm gonna get a lawyer" and a decision to file a lawsuit. Lawsuits are costly, the adversarial process is stressful for all persons involved, the results are uncertain, and litigation processes are not simple or easy to pursue (Franke 2000).

If you do end up in court, the claims that will typically be successful if litigation occurs include the denial of substantive due process challenging the "correctness" of the denial of tenure or where there are written promises of continued employment that create a property interest (Copeland and

Murray 1996). Generally speaking, where there is "competent and credible evidence to support the evaluator's decision" the courts will not modify the institutional decision (Copeland and Murray 1996: 258). The judicial deference given to the "academic" assessment of the quality of your work is a well-established legal principle (Dekat 2009).

If you receive unfavorable evaluations in your review processes prior to your tenure review, you should try to address any detected problems rather than either rejecting the evaluation out of hand or taking an adversarial approach. Your seeking clarification in meetings with the evaluators involved to obtain a clear understanding of the identified problems and also seeking opportunities to respond to any claimed deficiencies are essential responsive activities (remember to write that confirming follow-up email).

Some court challenges to negative tenure/promotion recommendations and decisions have been successful when they were based on procedural due process grounds (guaranteeing such rights as having a hearing, an impartial decision maker, reasonable notice of claimed deficiencies, and an opportunity to speak on their own behalf), although the due process standards are not as high for academic processes as they are for judicial proceedings (Dekat 2009). Challenges claiming that collegiality requirements were applied incorrectly have not been as successful, even where collegiality is not explicitly stated as a performance expectation (Adams 2006). The need to have proof that is admissible in court is why it was in your interests over the years of your employment to have consistently documented all parts of all your tenure and personnel reviews and to have consistently made reasonable efforts to seek clarity in your understanding of performance expectations, including documentation of that effort and any of the responses to those efforts (Copeland and Murray 1996). The use of alternative dispute resolution processes is an avenue that could also be explored, as litigation for the untenured faculty is a risky option. As Copeland and Murray note:

> Colleges and universities are not required by law to make intelligent personnel decisions, any more than a business is required to do so. Sometimes institutional decisions are well reasoned, reward meritorious performance, and reflect institutional needs. But institutions at times make ridiculous, short-sighted decisions almost totally lacking in careful reasoning and judgment. Colleges and universities are free to make bad personnel decisions, but they are not free to make illegal personnel decisions which violate constitutional and statutory rights of faculty.
>
> (1996: 327)

Finally, after the shock of any negative tenure decision has worn off, you should candidly assess your performance at your institution and, regardless of the merits of any challenge you might be able to bring, you should consider your third option. In this process you should consult with your mentors and explore the three options, including seriously considering if you really want to stay, regardless of the merits of any potential lawsuit or grievance. Do you want to pay the high costs – financial and emotional – of a lawsuit? What if you lose? Is this the place where you want to go to work when you get out of bed every day? Are these the people with which you want to spend your work life? Do you want to vindicate yourself in a lawsuit and then sit in a department meeting where you will be working with people who may have testified against you in a deposition or in court? The principal goal of a challenge to the denial of tenure administratively or by litigation is to obtain that status – is that really what you want for your work life (Perlmutter 2007)? Perhaps, in your case, your extrinsic worth might be more apparent and more valued in a different work setting. It is something that you should seriously consider. Regardless of the stigma that attaches as a result of the denial of tenure there is also stigma attached to bringing a lawsuit and to some degree to having challenged the decision through a grievance process – even where you are successful.

Conclusion

The structure of the tenure review process places you in a position of "abjection" to the "senior" faculty by virtue of your status as "junior" faculty (Williams 1999: 14). The process has the potential of placing you in a position of submission and it has inherent risks of abuse and humiliation very similar to the hazing practices of some college sororities and fraternities, which is a rite of passage that has been outlawed in many states. At its worst, this process that is intended to provide you with academic freedom "induces fear rather than freedom" and "is the enduring power cord of relations among academic workers, incorporating those who judge, as well as those who are judged" (Williams 1999: 15). It can be a cycle of abuse that extends beyond tenure concerns. Untenured faculty members do not even have a legally recognized right to a "name clearing hearing" (Mawdsley 1999: 168) in court if they are denied tenure unless they have the legal basis to exercise their option of bringing a civil lawsuit based on contractual or employment rights violations (Hora 2001).

The tenure process places the primary responsibilities on you. The burden is on you to show your worth, but you also have it within your power to take actions that make more certain that your performance as presented in your tenure materials will comply with your institutional and departmental tenure requirements by being your own advocate. Pay attention to the fact that getting tenure is your job and that performing well in your job will get you tenure. Seek out appropriate mentors, be open to opportunities for constructive criticism, know what is expected of you, document your fulfillment of those expectations, document communications, and become tenured.

Note

1 I'd like to thank Katherine Rodriguez for all for her hard work on this chapter.

References

Adams, M. L. (2006) "The quest for tenure: Job security and academic freedom," *Catholic University Law Review*, 56: 67–96.

American Council on Education (2000) *Good Practice In Tenure Evaluation*, Washington, DC: American Council on Education. Online. Available HTTP: <http//www.acenet.edu/bookstore/> (accessed November 13, 2004).

Austin, A. E., and Rice, R. E. (1998) "Making tenure viable: Listening to early career faculty," *American Behavioral Scientist*, 41 (5): 736–55. Online. Available through Proquest database (accessed November 6, 2004).

Bellas, M. L. (1999) "Emotional labor in academia: The case of professors," *Annals of the American Academy of Political and Social Science*, 561: 96–112. Online. Available through Lexis Academic Universe (accessed November 6, 2004).

Bogat, G. A., and Redner, R. L. (1985) "How mentoring affects the professional development of women in psychology," *Professional Psychology: Research and Practice*, 16 (6): 1–7. Online. Available through FirstSearch database (accessed November 11, 2004).

Bonner, F. A., II (2004) "Black professors: On the track but out of the loop," *Chronicle of Higher Education*, 50 (40): B11. Online. Available through Proquest database (accessed November 6, 2004).

Cloud, R. C. (1998) "Evaluating and revising tenure in higher education: Implications for practitioners," *West's Education Law Reporter*, 128: 931–37. Online. Available through Westlaw Campus database (accessed November 6, 2004).

Copeland, J. D., and J. W. Murray (1996) "Getting tossed from the ivory tower: The legal implications of evaluating faculty performance," *Missouri Law Review*, 61: 233–327. Online. Available through Westlaw Campus database (accessed November 6, 2004).

D.O.A. (1988) Film directed by Annabel Jankel and Rocky Morton, Burbank, CA: Touchstone Pictures.

Dekat, G. S. (2009) "John Jay, discrimination, and tenure," *St. Mary's Law Review on Minority Issues*, 11: 237–76.

Douglas, L., and A. George (2000) "Gaining tenure: Rules your chairman never told you," *Chronicle of Higher Education*, 46: B10. Online. Available through Proquest database (accessed November 6, 2004).

Finkin, M. W., and Post, R. C. (2009) *"For the Common Good": Principles of American Academic Freedom*, New Haven, CT: Yale University Press.

Fogg, P. (2003) "Widening the tenure track: A university offers some instructors an unusual level of job security, despite opposition," *Chronicle of Higher Education*, 49 (17): A8. Online. Available through Proquest database (accessed November 6, 2004).

Fogg, P. (2004) "Hello … I must be going," *Chronicle of Higher Education*, 50 (41): A10. Online. Available through Proquest database (accessed November 6, 2004).

Franke, A. H. (2000) "Why battles over tenure shouldn't end up in the courtroom," *Chronicle of Higher Education*, 46 (49): B6. Online. Available through Proquest database (accessed November 6, 2004).

Franke, A. H. (2001) "Making defensible tenure decisions," *Academe*, 87 (6): 32–37. Online. Available through Proquest database (accessed November 6, 2004).

Helms, M. M., Williams, A. B., and Nixon, J. C. (2001) "TQM principles and their relevance to higher education: The questions of tenure and post-tenure review," *International Journal of Educational Management*, 15 (6): 32–42. Online. Available through Proquest database (accessed November 6, 2004).

Hora, M. (2001) "The courts and academia: Tenure discrimination claims against colleges and universities," *Journal of Law and Education*, 30 (2): 349–57. Online. Available through Proquest database (accessed November 6, 2004).

Mawdsley, R. D. (1999) "Collegiality as a factor in tenure review," *Journal of Personnel Evaluation in Education*, 13 (2): 167–77. Online. Available through ABI/Inform database (accessed November 6, 2004).

Moody, J. (2000) "Tenure and diversity: Some different voices," *Academe*, 86 (3): 30–34. Online Available through Proquest database (accessed November 6, 2004).

Nelson, C. (1997) "The real problem with tenure is incompetent faculty hiring," *Chronicle of Higher Education*, 44 (12): B4–B5. Online. Available through Proquest database (accessed November 6, 2004).

Pedriolo, C. A. (2004) "A new image in the looking glass: Faculty mentoring, individual, invitational rhetoric and the second class status of women in U.S. Academia," *Hastings Women's Law Journal*, 15: 185–215.

Perlmutter, D. D. (2007) "You didn't get tenure. What now?," *Chronicle of Higher Education*, 53 (50): 64.

Sandler, B. R. (1992) "Success and survival strategies for women faculty members," Washington, DC: Association of American Colleges.

Sawislak, K. (1999) "Denying tenure: Who said anything about fairness?," *Chronicle of Higher Education*, 46 (4): B4–B7. Online. Available through Proquest database (accessed November 6, 2004).

Seldin, P. (2006) *Evaluating Faculty Performance: A Practical Guide to Assessing, Teaching, Research and Service*, San Francisco, CA: Anker.

Seldin, P., and Miller, E. J. (2008) *The Academic Portfolio: A Practical Guide to Documenting, Teaching, Research, and Service*, San Francisco, CA: Jossey-Bass.

Shea, R. H. (2002) "The new insecurity: Fewer and fewer professors actually get it, but tenure is still the coin of the realm," *U.S. News and World Report*, 132 (9): 40. Online. Available through Oxford (accessed November 6, 2004).

Siow, A. (1998) "Tenure and other unusual personnel practices in academia," *Journal of Law, Economics, and Organizations*, 14 (1): 152–73. Online. Available through Oxford Journals database (accessed November 6, 2004).

Steinpreis, R. E., Anders, K.A., and Ritzke, D. (1999) "The impact of gender on the review of the curricula vitae of job applicants and tenure candidates: A national empirical study," *Sex Roles*, 47 (7): 509–28.

Szeto, W. F., and Wright, P. C. (2003) "Searching for an ideal: A cross-disciplinary study of university faculty," *Equal Opportunities International*, 22 (8): 54–73. Online. Available through Proquest database (accessed November 6, 2004).

Wagner, E. N. (1991) "Tenure committees, take heed: University of Pennsylvania v. EEOC should change the way you proceed," *Education Law Reporter*, 64: 979–95. Online. Available through Westlaw Campus database (accessed October 25, 2004).

Williams, J. (1999) "The other politics of tenure," *College Literature*, 26 (3): 226–42. Online. Available through Proquest database (accessed November 6, 2004).

Wilson, R. (2001) "A higher bar for earning tenure," *Chronicle of Higher Education*, 47 (17): A12. Online. Available through Proquest database (accessed November 6, 2004).

Zirkel, P. A. (1999) "The personality problem," *Phi Delta Kappan*, 80 (8): 622–25. Online. Available through Proquest database (accessed November 6, 2004).

9 Retirement

Another frontier

Susan F. Sharp

All too often, retirement planning focuses solely or primarily on the economics of retirement. While ensuring adequate income is important, it is only one aspect of retirement.[1] As an academic and a woman, I find myself more concerned about navigating the psychological and emotional shoals of retirement. This chapter focuses on some of the more widely recognized issues as well as some that may not be often considered.

As I approach retirement age, I find myself thinking about how retirement will affect me. Therefore, when I had the opportunity to write this chapter, I was excited. It gave me an excuse to read the literature on the subject, which I quickly discovered was voluminous. It also gave me the chance to reflect on my own plans and how realistic they might be. Finally, it helped me begin to consider how we, as a society, define retirement.

Although at first glance retirement seems a simple concept, it can be defined in a number of ways (Henretta 1997). What exactly do we mean when we say someone is "retired"? Retirement does not simply mean that one is not employed. There are those in the population who, whether by choice or circumstance, do not work for pay (e.g., the unemployed, disabled, and full-time home makers). Retirement implies that one is retiring *from* something. However, simply leaving a job also does not constitute retirement. Instead, retirement is generally viewed as an *earned privilege* to no longer work full-time. Thus, retirement involves separation from a job or series of jobs, where the individual has worked long enough to achieve the status of former worker, with the guarantee of some income and benefits.

Retirement, as it is generally understood in the early twenty-first century, also implies a shift in work patterns rather than a complete termination of all work, as many individuals do not end paid employment upon retirement (Hardy and Quadagno 1995). Indeed, the majority of workers today phase out of the work force upon "retirement," working at least part-time for the first five years or so (Atchley 2000; Moynagh and Worsley 2006).

Finally, retirement suggests the development of a new identity, no longer based primarily on how one earns a living. In Western society, career or job is often a master status for the adult, particularly the professional adult. When asked what we do, our response is not that we teach or do research.

Instead, the tendency is to identify ourselves as professors or researchers. In retirement, we must forge a new identity. To successfully negotiate this transition, planning is helpful.

The evolution of retirement as a phase of the life course

Prior to industrialization, the concept of retirement did not exist as we know it today (Atchley 2000; Moen 2003; Moynagh and Worsley 2006). However, the industrial revolution brought about two changes that led to the emergence of a retirement system. First, industrialization created the need for fewer workers. At the same time, people were living longer due to improvements in health care and sanitation. Laws were enacted to preclude children entering the work force as well as to mandate that older workers leave the work force, although forced retirement due to age alone is now usually considered discriminatory. Nonetheless, retirement arose in part to prevent a surplus of workers. Second, the industrial revolution led to increased mobility and hence less reliance on the extended family system. Thus, the aging person was less likely to be living near or with family who would care for her. At the same time, the bureaucratic structure of the state was developing. The responsibility for the support of aging workers was thus transferred from the family to the government and other bureaucracies. The first known retirement system emerged in England during the early nineteenth century (Atchley 2000). In essence, a new life stage emerged (Moen 2003).

At the dawn of the new millennium, Western society is faced with a large cohort of potential retirees: the baby boomer generation. This has led to a number of concerns about how well existing social security and pension plans will be able to support such a large group of former workers. Increasing life expectancy (Cohen 2006), decreasing fertility rates and thus fewer current workers (Moynagh and Worsley 2006), and an economic downturn have added to these concerns. This has led to evolving and complex patterns of retirement (Henretta 1997; Moen 2003). One solution has been to encourage postponement of retirement. Laws prohibiting age discrimination and legislation overturning mandatory retirement requirements have emerged as a result. Another solution has been to encourage a slow phasing out of the work force. This has in turn led to changes in how eligibility for retirement is defined. For example, in 1996, my institution moved from the Rule of Eighty to the Rule of Ninety. In other words, those hired prior to the change were eligible to retire when the sum of their chronological age and years of service equaled eighty. For those hired after the policy change, the total had to equal ninety, effectively postponing retirement for newer workers. However, there is a caveat to this at my place of employment: all workers become eligible at age sixty-two, regardless of the sum of their ages and years of service to the institution.

One aspect of phasing workers out is the use of retirees as consultants or adjuncts (Alexander 2006). Under this model, you "retire" and then immediately or shortly thereafter return to the same institution, albeit in a transformed role.

The benefit for the institution, of course, is that there is no longer a require-ment to pay into the retirement fund of the individual or to provide benefits. The benefit to us is that we can remain involved in the field, continuing to mentor students and younger colleagues. The institution is able to benefit from the expertise and experience of the worker, but at a lesser cost (Alexander 2006).

It is interesting, from a scholarly standpoint, to see how retirement has evolved. Prior to the industrial revolution, people worked until they were no longer physically able to do so. At that point, the family stepped in and cared for the individual until death. With the breakdown in the extended family and the need for fewer workers, retirement began emerging only two centuries ago. By the middle of the twentieth century, thanks to programs like Social Security, it has become ubiquitous.

Now, with a smaller labor force having to carry the financial burden of a large retirement age population, new approaches are emerging. For those of you considering eminent retirement, this has opened up new avenues, including the phasing out of work over time. Choices now include working longer, moving to part-time work, becoming involved in volunteer work, increased leisure activities, or retiring from one career and working either full-time or part-time at another (Cox et al. 2006). After a brief examination of how gender may play into the choices, I will return to a more personal exploration of these options.

The effects of retirement

Ideally, retirement planning should begin relatively early in one's career. Realistically, however, most of us are not that concerned at age thirty about how we will live our lives when we are in our fifties, sixties or seventies. Although we begin making economic contributions to a retirement plan when we begin working, we are less likely to begin planning how we will spend our time or adjust to new roles at the end of our careers. The focus at the beginning of one's career is generally on achieving competence and promotions, and it is only after a number of years that one is able to relax and enjoy one's career. In fact, older workers tend to report higher levels of job satisfaction and commit-ment to work than younger workers, due primarily to less pressure to achieve (Hanlon 1986; McNeely 1988). Many of us, therefore, postpone thinking about retirement until we are relatively close to retirement age.

For some of us, work begins being seen as less desirable in our fifties. For example, Karp (1987) found that professional men experienced a sharp decline in job satisfaction at that age. This may reflect decreasing challenges in the work, which may seem more repetitive after one has mastered a profession or career. Conversely, with the rapid changes occurring today, it may reflect increasing challenges to update our older skills, staying abreast of new infor-mation and mastering new technologies.

Perhaps this applies less to our lives as academics, faced with the importance of staying abreast of continuous advancements in research and theory.

However, the academic may instead become somewhat disenchanted with the level of commitment required to stay current in the field, leading to a different type of dissatisfaction with work (Karp 1989). Some research supports this as a benefit of retirement, indicating that those who are retired report lower stress levels and better mental health than non-retired individuals of the same age (Midanik et al. 1995). It is noteworthy that the majority of people do not have a negative attitude about retiring, regardless of how satisfied they are with their jobs or careers (Karp 1987; Calasanti 1996; Atchley 2000). Those of us who do look negatively on retirement tend to either feel we have not yet achieved our professional goals or else have no firm idea about what to do once we retire (Karp 1989). This suggests the importance of planning for retirement, broadly defined. This planning is further shaped by our personal biographies (Moen 2003).

Interestingly, loss of the career role does not necessarily lead to loss of self-worth. Although early research suggested that leaving your career would lead to a loss of identity, this has not been unilaterally supported by later research (Reitzes et al. 1996). In part, how you view the effects of retirement depends on whether you adhere to the crisis theory of retirement or the continuity theory of retirement. Under the crisis model, your primary source of identity and well-being is linked to your career. Thus, retirement would be expected to lead to a crisis in identity. In contrast, continuity theory argues that retirement is in and of itself a respected role and thus a source of self-esteem (Calasanti 1996). Successful transitioning would thus depend on how well your other roles are increased or modified as employment is decreased. This indicates that, ideally, part of retirement planning should focus on increasing your commitment to roles other than work, over a period of time (Moen 2003).

Greene (2006) offers suggestions for how to make the transition into retirement with minimal upheaval. One important step is to realize that it is easy to over-commit yourself when faced with no work obligations. Some retirees fear that saying "No" may preclude further opportunities. However, to avoid stress, it is important to be selective, taking on only those jobs or projects that seem most important to you. Furthermore, giving yourself permission to simply do less is part of the learning experience. Since the time immediately preceding retirement can be extremely busy, the new retiree may want to take some time to simply relax before considering new alternatives (Greene 2006). Flexibility can be important, too. Once retired, you have the luxury of changing your plans as opportunities emerge.

Gender and retirement

Much of the extant research on retirement has been focused almost exclusively on men, as is true in most social science research. However, we are now faced with a large cohort of women who have worked throughout most of their adult lives, who are approaching retirement age. Some research suggests that retirement is even better for women than for men, in part because women are more likely to be doing most of the unpaid household labor while working at a paying job (Midanik et al. 1995). However, other research suggests that women fare worse after retiring than men, perhaps due to loss of relationships associated with employment (Kim and Moen 2002).

Retirement planning for men and women, however, differs, in part because of the lower earning power of women in the work force. Women earn less than men on average, and retirement pensions are linked to overall earnings. This may then affect the age at which women plan to retire. Recent research suggests that this may not be as problematic as you might think, however. It is not the age of retirement that is the greatest predictor of satisfaction. Instead, it is the degree to which your retirement coincides with the planned age of retirement (Moen 2003). For women, firm retirement plans are linked to race, work history and marital status (Wong and Hardy 2009). The effect of race is probably linked to the employment sector where women of color are concentrated. Stable retirement plans are associated with longer and more stable work histories and adequate retirement pensions. Likewise, being married tends to be linked to more concrete plans for retirement, probably at least in part due to having adequate resources to ensure a comfortable retirement (Wong and Hardy 2009).

As academics and practitioners, most individuals reading this volume are employed in the primary job sector. However, lifetime earnings have quite possibly been impacted by having children, and many of us have gone in and out of the labor market or postponed working towards promotions due to child care concerns. Thus, our anticipated retirement incomes may be lower than those of many of our male peers (Calasanti 1996). On the other hand, women tend to derive more life satisfaction from their children, so even though our retirement incomes may have been negatively affected, this is counterbalanced by the role that our grown children and their families may have in our retirement plans (Calasanti 1996).

Additionally, having a spouse who is retiring may be linked to women's retirement plans, as couples tend to coordinate the time of retirement (Moen 2003; Szinovacz and DeViney 1999). If women retire after their husbands, this can lead to renegotiation of household duties. If the woman continues working, she may rightfully anticipate her husband will do the majority of the domestic chores, but this is not always realized. In fact, research indicates that having your spouse retire is linked to higher satisfaction for men than for women (Moen 2003). Additionally, increased marital conflict is common in couples with one spouse retired and one still working (Kim and Moen 2002; Moen 2003). This may be particularly true when the woman is still working and the man is retired. Household labor probably still falls primarily to the woman. She may rightfully resent working both inside and outside the home while her spouse does neither.

Of course, children and spouses are not the only individuals that are important in our lives. For most of us, work also means the development of long-term relationships with coworkers. Upon retirement, many of these relationships will change or even fade away. However, women tend to be more fortunate than men in this aspect, as they are usually more networked into their communities, providing a wider range of friends (Moen 2003). Volunteer activities provide a potential source of friendships to replace work relationships (Kim and Moen 2002; Moen 2003). Regardless of the source, though, it is important to have social networks in place during the transition into retirement.

Retirement planning from a personal perspective

A few years ago, I got a lesson from a colleague in how *not* to retire. His experience taught me the importance of having a strong network of friends and activities in place well in advance of retirement. This colleague had spent his entire adult life building his reputation as a scholar and teacher. He was a prolific researcher and highly respected professor at the university where we worked. Unfortunately, he had very few outside interests. In fact, other than time spent with his son, he had virtually no outside interests. He was faced with sudden retirement due to a negative health event, and he suddenly had a huge hole in his life. Since that time, he has made no effort to reengage with the academic community or the community in which we live, and he spends his days alone. Initially, his colleagues and former students tried to include him in activities, but he showed little interest in anything. He bemoaned the loss of identity that accompanied his forced retirement. His mental health has deteriorated rather quickly. He is now reclusive and often will not answer either his door or his telephone. As I prepared to write this chapter, I called him to see if he had adjusted any better. He told me he was miserable and stayed home all the time, rarely talking with people.

I learned a number of lessons from watching him. Perhaps the most important one was that retirement planning should start well before actual retirement. In his case, the actual time of retirement was not planned. However, he had already planned to retire within a year or so of the date he had the health problems, but it was obvious he had not considered what he would do with his time. The literature does suggest that unplanned retirement due to layoffs, downsizing, or health problems is linked to higher levels of dissatisfaction with retirement (Calasanti 1996; Moen 2003). In my colleague's case, physical recovery from his health crisis did occur, but mental recovery appears to not have happened. Thus, while he has relatively good health and an excellent income, the loss of structure and relationships associated with his career has been overwhelming.

Pondering how to avoid the same pitfall, I began examining my own life. What portion of my time did I spend in work activities? Where could I add other activities? What work activities might carry over into my retirement? In my case, the answer was to become more involved in the community at large, carrying my research to interested parties in my city and state. I had already established a network of practitioners interested in my work. However, I had not taken as much time to develop ties with social activists. Therefore, over the past three years, I have been actively integrating my work into my life in the community, developing new friendships as well as strengthening existing ones.

This has taken some investigation and effort on my part, especially in the initial stages. In order to find out where to best invest my time and energy, I have investigated a number of different groups, seeking the best fit. Now, I am very active in a group of social activists with interests that overlap with mine. There have been a number of fringe benefits. Not only do I have a plan for how to spend my time, but I also have a number of new friends with interests similar to my own. This has led to new goals and planned activities. I am in the initial stages of formulating a plan for a nonprofit organization to assist women prisoners in reintegrating into the community, and I hope to devote more of my energy to this endeavor as I close in on retirement. My involvement with this group has also broadened my areas of interest. Their goal is to work directly on social justice issues, broadly defined. Rather than limiting my involvement to only those areas of my own expertise, I have been challenged to learn about new and equally important problems in the community. Therefore, active involvement in the community is one important part of my preretirement planning.

As a college professor, my work has entailed a number of different aspects: research, teaching/mentoring and service. As a retiree, this will shift. Probably, less of my time will be spent doing research and mentoring students, although I will still continue doing some research. Teaching will shift. I anticipate continuing to teach but to play a background role rather than a leadership role. However, service may take on a new and different role in my life. Service takes many different forms, and I have always contributed my time to a number of different things. Where my energy is devoted will shift as I retire, but I intend to remain very active in criminal justice initiatives in my state. Additionally, I am becoming more interested in new types of service. The community group that I have been involved with over the past year or so includes community gardening as one of its many social justice issues. I am intrigued enough to plan on devoting time to this project now. After retirement, I plan to become more involved in the community garden project as a way of promoting nutrition, shared responsibility, and a stronger sense of community.

Teaching and mentoring also have their places in my plans for retirement. One of the perquisites of being a college professor is the opportunity to continue teaching. My university has a number of options open to me. There is, of course, emeritus teaching, wherein I can continue teaching a small number of courses for my department. However, that is only one avenue open to me. We also have an expansive continuing education college that offers courses through a number of departments. I have taught actively in those programs for years, and I plan to continue doing so. Although universities differ, many will have some version of this available. One of the benefits is that you can frequently teach a specialty course that is not regularly offered in your home department.

There are also opportunities to teach at other places. In larger communities, there may be several universities or community colleges. Adjunct faculty members are often the backbone of smaller colleges. Establishing relationships with those institutions prior to retirement is a good idea if you think you would like to teach for them. Personally, I have considered a different option to ease me out of the academy. The first semester after retirement, I hope to teach at another institution as a visiting faculty member. I have discussed this possibility with friends at other institutions, and I am reasonably optimistic that I will be able to do this. This would serve a couple of purposes. First, it would provide me with a bridge into retirement. I could still be actively teaching, but I would not have the other responsibilities that I have at my current institution. Second, by putting myself in a different locale, I believe that I will be less acutely aware that I am no longer mentoring graduate students.

The loss of the mentoring role will be one of the more difficult challenges for me. Being an academic is a second career for me, and my active involvement with graduate students has been one of the hallmarks of my tenure at my institution. Like my recently retired and not so happy colleague, part of my identity has been intricately involved in being a mentor. I recognize that this will be problematic for me, and I am currently investigating other ways of mentoring. While it may not come with as much recognition or as many kudos, mentoring disadvantaged school-age children is one option. I would like to volunteer my time at the local high school to try to entice some of the less advantaged adolescents into learning. I have also begun the preretirement process by slowly easing out of my mentorship role. I no longer take on new doctoral students, and I serve on fewer graduate student committees. It is my plan to be almost totally out of this role before I actually retire so that I feel the loss less keenly.

One of the most important ways we can plan for retirement is through honestly assessing ourselves. I have spent the past year asking myself, "What are my greatest strengths? What are my weaknesses? How will those manifest when I leave the paid work force?" This is not a process for the weak, as I have had to digest some rather unpleasant truths about myself, chief of which has been that I really like to receive recognition and praise! I strongly encourage anyone contemplating retirement to face those inner demons. Referring again to my retired colleague, I have seen at first hand the devastation caused by not recognizing and owning one's own shortcomings. If he had developed the self-awareness that leaving his career would eliminate the source of much of his self-worth, perhaps he could have better prepared himself. I, on the other hand, will not be surprised by how this loss affects me. While I do not believe the process will be painless, I think that knowing this is going to be a loss will help me recognize and deal with the feelings as they arise.

Conclusion

Retirement should be considered a process, not an event. In the early twenty-first century, retirement is often characterized by a slow process of leaving the work force. Careful preretirement planning can ease the transition into the world of retirement. While ensuring adequate income is important, the emotional aspects may be even more difficult.

My advice to those contemplating retirement is to begin this process several years in advance of the targeted retirement date. The initial step should be an honest assessment of oneself. This should incorporate not only an evaluation of how you spend your time but also the ways different parts of your work are tied to your self-worth. Then, begin preparing yourself for the future absence of that role. This means looking for new sources of self-worth, whether those be gardening, painting, or something academic.

In addition, start laying the groundwork for transitional employment. Since many people phase out of the work force, it is helpful to explore the ways in which you might be able to do this in your own institution or through other institutions. This means careful examination of the policies and opportunities open to you. This also involves an honest assessment of where your own contributions might be most welcomed. For those of us in the academy or who have had careers as researchers, consulting work and teaching are two easily identifiable areas of transitional employment.

Find out what opportunities exist for retired faculty to teach occasional courses in your department or institution. Explore this possibility at other institutions in the area. Consider taking visiting teaching jobs at other institutions. There are many different options available to those of us who would like to continue to teach.

Begin developing new networks or strengthening existing ones. As you move closer to your projected retirement date, shift your time and energy towards those activities that will become more important when you actually retire.

Last and not least, be honest with yourself. Forewarned is indeed forearmed. Awareness of what parts of this transition may be most difficult for you can help you put into place plans that can ameliorate the detrimental aspects of retirement. In my case, recognition that the loss of the mentoring role will be difficult has led me to begin easing out of mentoring activities well in advance of actual retirement. It has also led to reflection about the natural flow into different stages of life. By being less involved in the mentoring of graduate students, I am also allowing other colleagues to be more involved. I am also becoming busier in other areas of my life that will be taking up more and more of my time during my own movement into the ranks of the retired. I find that by developing new interests as well as modifying existing ones, I am becoming quite excited about approaching this new frontier of life: the ranks of the retired. Retirement does not have to mean loss of value or sense of contribution. It does mean realizing that my contributions may become more in the background, less recognized, but still fulfilling.

Note

1 Susan Caringella's AAUP retirement workshop highly recommends a series of books published by Wiley: John C. Bogle, *The Little Book of Common Sense Investing*

(2007); Christopher H. Browne, *The Little Book of Value Investing* (2007); David M. Darst, *The Little Book that Saves your Assets* (2007); Pat Dorsey, *The Little Book that Builds Wealth* (2008); Joel Greenblatt, *The Little Book that Beats the Market* (2006); Louis Navellier, *The Little Book that Makes you Rich* (2007).

References

Alexander, K. (2006) "Retired, but still on the job," in H. Cox (ed.) *Annual Editions: Aging*, 18th edn, Dubuque, IA: McGraw-Hill/Dushkin.

Atchley, R. C. (2000) *Social Forces and Aging*, 9th edn, Belmont, CA: Wadsworth.

Calasanti, T. M. (1996) "Gender and life satisfaction in retirement: An assessment of the male model," *Journal of Gerontology*, 51B: S18–S29.

Cohen, N. (2006) "Will they still need you, will they still feed you … when you're 64?," in H. Cox (ed.) *Annual Editions: Aging*, 18th edn, Dubuque, IA: McGraw-Hill/Dushkin.

Cox, H., Parks, T, Hammonds, A., and Sekhon, G. (2006) "Work/retirement choices and lifestyles of older Americans," in H. Cox (ed.) *Annual Editions: Aging*, 18th edn, Dubuque, IA: McGraw-Hill/Dushkin.

Gall, T. L., Evans, D. R., and Howard, J. (1997) "The retirement adjustment process: Changes in the well-being of male retirees across time," *Journal of Gerontology*, 52B: P110–P117.

Greene, K. (2006) "How to survive the first year," in H. Cox (ed.) *Annual Editions: Aging*, 18th edn, Dubuque, IA: McGraw-Hill/Dushkin.

Hanlon, M. (1986) "Age and commitment toward work," *Research on Aging*, 8: 289–316.

Hardy, M. A. and Quadagno, J. (1995). "Satisfaction with early retirement: Making choices in the auto industry," *Journal of Gerontology*, 50B: S217–S218.

Henretta, J. C. (1997) "Changing perspectives on retirement," *Journal of Gerontology*, 52B: S1–S3.

Karp, D. A. (1987) "Professional beyond midlife: Some observations on work satisfaction in the fifty-to-sixty decade," *Journal of Aging Studies*, 1: 209–24.

Karp, D. A. (1989) "The social construction of retirement among professionals 50–60 years old," *Gerontologist*, 29: 750–60.

Kim, J. E. and Moen, P. (2002) Retirement transitions, gender and psychological well-being: A life-course, ecological model," *Journal of Gerontology*, 57B: P212–P222.

McNeely, R. I. (1988) "Age and job satisfaction in human service employment," *Gerontologist*, 28: 163–68.

Midanik, L. T., Soghikian, K., Ransom, L. J., and Tekawa, I. S. (1995) "The effect of retirement on mental health and health behaviors: The Kaiser Permanente retirement study," *Journal of Gerontology*, 51B: S59–S61.

Moen, P. (2003) "Midcourse: Navigating retirement and a new life stage," in J. T. Mortimer and M. J. Shanahan (eds) *Handbook of the Life Course*, New York: Kluwer/Plenum.

Moynagh, M., and Worsley, R. (2006) "Reshaping retirement: Scenarios and options," in H. Cox (ed.) *Annual Editions: Aging*, 18th edn, Dubuque, IA: McGraw-Hill/Dushkin.

Reitzes, D. C., Mutran, E. J., and Fernandez, M. E. (1996) "Preretirement influences on postretirement self-esteem," *Journal of Gerontology*, 51B: S242–S249.

Szinovacz, M. E., and DeViney, S. (1999) "The retiree identity: Gender and race differences," *Journal of Gerontology*, 54B: S207–S218.

Wong, J. D., and Hardy, M. A. (2009) "Women's retirement expectations: How stable are they?," *Journal of Gerontology*, 64B: 77–86.

Conclusion
And the journey continues

There are many lessons that are thematic in these pages that traverse so many different waters which ebb and flow around an academic journey. Some of the most salient to us are, first, to prepare, strategize, develop a plan of attack, and organize the activities pertaining to your career, i.e., have a vision and plan for making it a reality. Second, set aside time, as you would with any other project, to gather knowledge about the requirements, processes, experiences, advice, and feedback of others. Third, muster, utilize, and grow the resources all around you that can work to support and further your achievements. Maintain and strengthen relationships with family, friends, and colleagues. Seek out mentors, develop your own networks, integrate into and build upon the networks of others. Fourth, prioritize your projects to manage your time in and out of the academy, and negotiate with others to get what you want, whether this is a salary, release research time, or time and/or understanding with family, friends, and colleagues. Balance your activities, your academic involvements and your 'outside' life. Women especially need to take care of themselves, like they take care of others. No one is going to do *any* of this for you. Further, realize that turnaround is fair play – give back to those who facilitate you, facilitate others yourself, contribute to academic and other communities with the enthusiasm that comes from knowing that your work can make a difference. And finally, start this process *now:* it is never too early or too late to facilitate your own successes in realizing your goals, hopes and dreams.

While all of that which is encompassed in these chapters may seem intimidating or overwhelming, especially to the newest of comers to the profession, you need to bear in mind that what is offered in this book is the cumulative result of many, many years of development and experience by some of the most well-respected scholars (who, not incidentally, all voice that they wish a book like this had been available to them at earlier stages of their journeys) and all of the colleagues that influenced them, across a variety of institutions. This book simultaneously encompasses the duration of an academic career spanning what are literally decades upon decades for those of us, most of us, who stay with it all life long. This is to say too that most of us succeed; and make an enjoyable life and decent living revolving around reading, writing, thinking, talking, sharing, bringing along, and forming new generations of citizens and scholars, and breaking new ground through research and publications, contributing to society, and more, to make our living. And we get to largely structure our own time in so doing – a unique benefit in the academy (in spite of the occupational hazard of getting to structure our forty-plus, fifty-plus, sixty-plus hours a week in any way we want). Despite the roadblocks – roadblocks that you should by now see as surmountable, roadblocks that you now have strategies to overcome – the academic life provides wonderful opportunities at every turn too; what a great job!

Buddhism tells us that, where the mind goes, energy follows. Plan and work for your own successful academic future. We all think it is "way" worth it!

Index